SACRAMENTO

CREATIVE SOUL OF THE CITY

WILLIAM BURG

Charleston · London

THE
History
PRESS

Published by The History Press
Charleston, SC 29403
www.historypress.net

Front cover, top left to bottom right: Center for Sacramento History, *Suttertown News* collection; Mickey Abbey; John Muheim; Center for Sacramento History, *Suttertown News* collection; George Westcott; Jodette Johnson.

Back cover, top left to bottom right: Tara Elizabeth; Dane Henas; Heidi Bennett.

First published 2014

Manufactured in the United States

ISBN 978.1.62619.673.5

Library of Congress CIP data applied for.

Dedicated to the memory of four Midtown giants: James Henley, historian, archivist and founder of the Center for Sacramento History, 1944–2014; Jose Montoya, artist, poet and founding member of the Royal Chicano Air Force, 1932–2013; Brooks Truitt, neighborhood activist, hell-raiser and editor of the Old City Guardian, *1925–2014; and Socorro Zuniga, mother, social worker, artist and founding member of* Las Co-Madres Artistas, *1925–2014.*

Contents

Acknowledgements

This book is far from complete or comprehensive, and every chapter could easily be its own book—or several books. It culminates the story begun in my two previous books, *Sacramento's K Street* and *Sacramento Renaissance*. Each may be read separately, but they share common themes and characters. Thank you to those I interviewed for this book, including John Baccigaluppi, Heidi Bennett, Doug Biggert, James and Delphine Cathcart, Marco Fuoco, Brian Gorman, Diane Heinzer, Tim Holt, David Houston, Mayor Phil Isenberg, Donnie Jupiter, Stewart Katz, Dale Kooyman, Susan Larson, Stan Lunetta, Mark Miller, Joan Riordan, David Rolin, Mayor Anne Rudin, Kevin Seconds, Jodette Silhi, Esteban Villa, Dennis Yudt and Socorro Zuniga. Scott Soriano provided firsthand accounts, primary source material and peer review of the manuscript. Some information and quotes came from Sacramento-oriented Facebook groups, including Vintage Sacramento, Things I Remember Growing Up in Sacramento, Original Sactown OG Punk Rockers United and Tales of Terror.

Many of the photos in this book come from two talented photographers who documented Sacramento in the 1970s through the 1990s. Joe Perfecto captured street scenes as a freelance photographer for *Suttertown News* and the *Old City Guardian*. His lens captured a human element of Downtown Sacramento street life. John Muheim specialized in music photography, documenting well-known performers at Cal Expo and Memorial Auditorium and local punk bands at small venues like Club Minimal, capturing the spirit and energy of a little-documented scene. Other photos were provided

Bobby Burns at the 1997 Heritage Festival. Bobby was well known in Midtown, a talented percussionist with a unique dress style. *Photo by Allyson Seconds.*

by Mara Wagner, Melissa Hays, Dane Henas, Allyson Seconds, Robert McKeown, William Peterson and Tara Elizabeth. Tim Foster provided photos taken by George Westcott.

Archives consulted for this book include the Center for Sacramento History, the California State Library's California Room, the Sacramento Public Library's microfilm collections and Sacramento Room, and the Lavender Library Archives and Cultural Exchange. Archivists Rebecca Crowther and Patricia Johnson guided me to photos from the enormous CSH collection. *Suttertown News* founder, Tim Holt, created a permanent record of a neighborhood's emergence, providing enormous insight into Midtown's story.

Much of this book is based on my own experiences living in Midtown Sacramento and participating in its interlocking communities, including nightlife and live music, coffee shop culture, arts and theater, historic preservation and neighborhood activism. My first visits to Midtown took place during the 1980s, a two-hour ride on bus and light rail from Citrus Heights. Arriving on K Street or Capitol Avenue, I became a *flâneur*, one who strolls the city with no purpose other than to enjoy city life. The streets and buildings, trees, goods sold in the stores—especially the people—all captured my eye and fired my imagination. I resolved to move there one day in order to avoid that two-hour ride and experience the neighborhood as a resident and full-time *flâneur*. When my friend Tania Morgan encouraged me to move into a Midtown punkhouse with seven roommates in late 1993, I jumped at the chance. Spending time at Midtown cafés and parties, I occasionally encountered a beautiful, brilliant young woman named Vivian Gerlach and, in 1996, worked up the nerve to introduce myself. In 1999, we were married in McKinley Park's Clunie Hall and walked home. We still enjoy strolling around Midtown on a mutual journey of discovery and exploration, a pleasure that increases when shared.

Introduction

Aliens in Our Midst

Star Trek *was an attempt to say that humanity will reach maturity and wisdom
on the day that it begins not just to tolerate, but* [to] *take a special delight in
differences in ideas and differences in life forms...If we cannot learn to actually
enjoy those small differences, to take a positive delight in those small differences
between our own kind, here on this planet, then we do not deserve to go out into
space and meet the diversity that is almost certainly out there.*
—Gene Roddenberry

In 1976, Sacramento had the largest *Star Trek* fan club in the world.
According to Terry Whittier—editor of *Stardate*, newsletter of the
Sacramento Valley chapter of the Star Trek Association for Revival, or
S.T.A.R.—*Star Trek* was "the only recent television show that treated science
fiction in an adult, painstakingly authentic, highly entertaining manner by
craftsmen who (because of their dedication and skill) make the future come
alive." Based on creator Gene Roddenberry's statements and the show's
groundbreaking representation of racial and gender diversity (including
actors Nichelle Nichols and George Takei and writers like Dorothy Fontana)
the show appealed to audiences coming of age during the 1960s who were
acutely aware of these issues. The civil rights, women's rights, gay liberation,
counterculture and anti-authoritarian movements of this era dominated
public discourse, and many of these narratives were addressed by science
fiction that transcended the genre's association with escapism and fantasy.[1]

But why did *Star Trek* find such popularity in Sacramento? When
acknowledged at all, Sacramento is associated with regional agriculture,

Star Trek fan art from *STARDATE*, Sacramento STAR newsletter. *Robert McKeown collection.*

gold rush heritage and state government, or it is viewed as a stop on the way to Lake Tahoe. Its bucolic suburban neighborhoods are seldom associated with dramatic social change, high technology or interest in the future, leading one local writer to refer to Sacramento neighborhoods like Land Park as "a hotbed of civil rest."[2] The answer lies in a postwar cultural shift in Sacramento's economics that produced more artists, who concentrated in Midtown. Geographically located on the eastern half of Sacramento's old central city grid, this neighborhood emerged in the wake of Downtown Sacramento's redevelopment era in the 1970s, with the name "Midtown" entering the city's lexicon around 1983. The term differentiates the mixed-use residential neighborhoods surrounding Downtown Sacramento from the central business district. Newspaper editor Tim Holt used the term

"Suttertown" to describe Midtown, calling it more of a state of mind than a geographic area.[3]

In *Neo-Bohemia: Art and Commerce in the Postindustrial City*, sociologist Richard Lloyd explored how Wicker Park grew from a working-class Chicago neighborhood into a bohemian district. This transition occurred because of changes in the American workplace resulting from the wealth and mass culture of postwar America. Between 1900 and 1999, the percentage of Americans who identified themselves as artists, writers and performers tripled. In 1900, only 267 Americans per 100,000 identified themselves in this category. Until 1960, that number grew only slightly, to 336 per 100,000. In 1970, the figure jumped to 385, then to 565 in 1980—twice as many creative workers per capita—and to 784 in 1991. In 1999, the number reached 900, a tripling of the proportion of artists in the American workplace.

With greater proportions of artists, bohemian neighborhoods appeared outside the traditional big-city centers in cities like Austin, Minneapolis, Cleveland, Detroit, Portland, Chicago, Denver and Sacramento. All were former industrial cities whose neighborhoods took on new roles as postmodern cities emerged. Lloyd also argued that artists were not randomly distributed throughout those cities. They preferred old city centers, even in struggling cities, creating what Lloyd called a "networked geography of cultural production." When artists were scarcer, major cities were the only places with enough artists to create networks of resources and social connections necessary to support an art market. As the number of artists grew, artists could form their own networks in smaller cities if they stayed geographically close enough to meet one another. Bohemian neighborhoods like Midtown combine physical places and cultural practices. Their borders are not always distinct, and not everyone who lives within those borders, or even a majority of them, is a bohemian. But they become a recognizable presence that shapes the neighborhood's identity.[4]

Midtown was the point where the redevelopers' bulldozers stopped and Sacramento's older architectural legacy survived. Changes in California's economy, a growing awareness of the consequences of redevelopment and action by civil rights advocates slowed the demolition of Sacramento's Old City in the 1960s, but the damage to Downtown Sacramento was already fatal. The survival of Midtown was based on its location. Sacramento's role as a transportation hub dates back to the Gold Rush. The foot of K Street became the last stop for Argonauts bound for the central mines, the inland stop for riverboats and the center of stagecoach, Pony Express, telegraph and railroad networks that radiated from Sacramento, not San Francisco, to reach the state's hinterlands and east across the Sierra Nevada. By the mid-twentieth century, Sacramento retained its role as a transportation hub via highways, airfields and telecommunications networks. Sacramento's dispersed regional growth, like that of larger cities like Los Angeles, created a metropolitan regional identity that stretched from the Sierra Nevada foothills into the Sacramento River Delta, a postmodern city without a center. Redevelopment and depopulation left a social vacuum at the city's heart. Because Downtown's housing was gone, the college students, counterculture hippies, gays and lesbians, young professionals and artists seeking a home in the city's core moved to Midtown. Lacking a regional center, they created their own in a neighborhood left for dead. Midtown emerged at this confluence of place and ideas, creating the networked geography of cultural production where the arts could survive and thrive.

SOMETHING TO DO WITH ROCKETS

Aerojet and Air Force Bases

Joan Didion's essay "Notes from a Native Daughter" was written as an epitaph for the Sacramento she knew. For Didion, Sacramento's true character was based in its agricultural roots and the close connections between the long-established families of Sacramento's upper class, whose wealth derived from farming interests around the city and throughout the Sacramento Valley. Often, the scions of these families lived in Sacramento, in first-ring streetcar suburbs like Land Park or, like Didion's family, around Poverty Ridge, Midtown's only hill, centered at Twenty-second and T Streets. They seldom tilled the soil, leaving that work to the migrant laborers of the West End, but referred to themselves as farmers to remind their children of the family's essential connection to the land and the rivers.[5]

As these families sold their agricultural holdings for new suburban tracts, they lost their power in the same way that the Los Angeles *californios* had a century earlier, exchanging their agricultural birthright for short-term economic gain. For Didion, their shift into cultural irrelevance marked the loss of Sacramento's character, the city's soul, but she ignored the birth of new souls in the suburban tracts that once bore hops and grain. The new Sacramento middle class was unconcerned with the sacrifices of the Donner Party or membership in the Sutter Club. They arrived in the wake of the Second

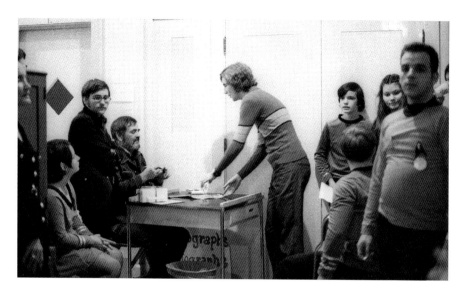

Star Trek fans at a Sacramento science fiction convention seeking autographs from James Doohan. *Photo by Joe Perfecto.*

World War or were the descendants of less wealthy classes of Sacramentans. Their eyes were on the future and their interests in the sky and stars, not the soil. Their children were equally unencumbered by earthly baggage.

The landing places for these new Sacramentans were suburban tracts laid out atop the old farmland to the south and east of Sacramento. Two of the most important land development firms, identified by CSUS graduate student Brian Roberts, were Wright & Kimbrough and Jones, Brand & Hullin. Owned by the same sort of old Sacramento families identified by Didion, both firms were important members of the Sacramento Chamber of Commerce. These firms and the chamber saw military investment as the key to Sacramento's future as early as 1932, when the U.S. War Department closed down Mather Field, a small facility used to train army pilots that was underutilized after 1918. In response to the airfield's closure, chamber of commerce secretary-manager Arthur Dudley led a regional effort to reopen Mather. In 1935, California senator Hiram Johnson, a native Sacramentan and former California governor, urged the Senate to reestablish Mather Field as part of the Wilcox Bill, a $200 million national program to establish new air bases. The bill also included funding for a second base outside Sacramento, established in 1939 as the Sacramento Army Air Depot, later known as McClellan Field. Sacramento's regional boosters also pursued public dollars

Beers Books, the oldest surviving bookstore in Sacramento, moved several times. This location is at Thirteenth and J Streets. *Photo by Joe Perfecto.*

for improved flood control as part of the Central Valley Project, making the new eastern suburbs less subject to flooding. The chamber of commerce routinely opposed funding via Depression-era public works agencies like the Works Progress Administration, but federal dollars for military bases and flood control were acceptable sources of revenue for the Sacramento elite.[6]

World War II drew enormous amounts of men and money to both air bases, and the Cold War ensured their continued importance to the region. The war also brought the Army Signal Depot to Sacramento, initially located in the Bercut-Richards cannery north of Downtown, relocated after the war to a facility on Sacramento's eastern edge. The private military-industrial complex, funded by government contracts, arrived in the form of Aerojet-General, opening a facility in eastern Sacramento County in 1950. Didion described Aerojet and its fifteen thousand employees, none whom she knew, as something so remote from the experience of longtime Sacramentans that they described its function as simply "something to do with rockets."[7]

PEOPLE WHO READ THINGS

Joan Didion's *Run, River* presented a fictionalized story of an old Sacramento family who, in 1959, subdivided their family farmland into suburbs. Using the character of the family's eldest son, Didion criticized the older generation's failure to recognize change when the son's mother asked him to buy her some new paperback books in Berkeley.

> *She did not seem to realize that there were now paperback bookstores in Sacramento. She and his father would never seem to get it through their heads that things were changing in Sacramento, that Aerojet-General and Douglas Aircraft and even the State College were bringing in a whole new class of people, people who had lived back East, people who read things.*

Sacramento never lacked bookstores, as indicated by *Suttertown News* columnist Lloyd Bruno. His preferred haunts of the 1920s and 1930s were Levinson's Books, founded in 1911, where fine books were available for as little as eighty cents, and the United Cigar Store at Eighth and K, which sold rag-paper editions remaindered from Brentano's in New York. Bruno rode Downtown on the No. 6 streetcar from Oak Park, searching for books, and records at the Sherman Clay music store on Twelfth and K. Paperback books, according to Didion an unknown commodity in Sacramento until the late 1950s, were not the medium of fine literature like Brentano's hardbound editions.[8] Paperbacks were artifacts of popular culture, including detective novels and science fiction. Mass production and distribution brought new ideas that took hold in the minds of young readers, even if they had to take a special trip Downtown to find them.

> *One of my earliest memories is going to Beers Bookstore. I was maybe twelve years old, they were one of the only stores in town that had back issues of comic books. They had pulp science fiction digest magazines and a good spin rack of current science fiction, it was one of my favorite stores…It was a journey to get Downtown. The buses didn't go out to where I lived at all, I had to walk a couple miles to get the bus or get a ride from somebody. It was the ultimate destination. I went to matinées at the Crest, the Fox and the Alhambra Downtown. They had kid matinees pretty much every week at the theaters, all the new monster movies for thirty-five cents!*
> —Donnie Jupiter

Many of the new suburban settlers were returning veterans who sought education via the GI Bill. Prior to the 1950s, higher education in Sacramento was limited to Sacramento Junior College or the University of California's College of Agriculture in Davis, ten miles west of Sacramento.

Governor Edmund G. "Jerry" Brown took office in 1974. His administration and personal style were influential to many Sacramentans, from his policies to his choice of residence. *Center for Sacramento History,* Suttertown News *collection.*

The postwar era brought California State University Sacramento, founded on the junior college campus in 1947 but expanding to its own campus in 1952–53, and Davis became a University of California general campus in 1959. These new schools represented a break from Didion's era, when college meant either Berkeley or Stanford. Regional universities provided greater educational opportunities for the newly arrived migrants and their children, and faculty jobs that attracted educated people. Both schools emphasized technical subjects, including engineering and physical sciences, and UC Davis struggled to overcome its "aggie" reputation by bolstering its art and music departments, drawing internationally recognized talent. CSUS gained its own cadre of artists, including Wayne Thiebaud, who first came to Sacramento as a soldier at Mather Field painting bomber nose art, subsequently teaching at Sacramento Junior College and UC Davis.

UC Davis also had KDVS, a student- and volunteer-run campus radio station whose first FM broadcasts began in January 1968 on 90.3 FM. As a student-run station, KDVS had a diverse and free-form style. In 1969, KDVS hosted a live call-in show with Governor Ronald Reagan, interviewed Angela Davis on the air, covered an all-day Vietnam War protest on the UC Davis campus and ran an Alsatian for 1969 Homecoming Queen. The station upgraded from ten to five thousand watts in 1977, enough power to reach Sacramento audiences. Aside from a short-lived effort in 1983 to turn KDVS into a block-programmed Top 40 station, it retained its free-form ethos, with shows ranging the spectrum from classical, jazz and public affairs to reggae, punk and experimental music.[9]

American River College began as Grant Technical College in North Sacramento, relocating to a new campus in Cameron Ranch east of Sacramento in 1958. ARC became part of the Los Rios Community College district, providing low-cost vocational education to the region. By 1976, ARC also became the headquarters for the Star Trek fan club Sacramento STAR.

These new educational facilities, federally funded employment centers and high technology industries planted in the fertile soil of Sacramento County resulted in a bumper crop of children raised in Sacramento's postwar prosperity. The first two generations of this new suburban breed were collectively known as the baby boomers, born from the end of World War II until the early 1960s, and Generation X, those born up until 1980. Many of these young people, raised in the suburbs and seldom venturing Downtown, discovered the ruins of an old city around Sutter's Fort and began to explore it, intrigued by how different it was from the shopping malls and autocentric boulevards they knew.

Jerry Brown, Hipster in Chief

In 1974, Edmund G. "Jerry" Brown Jr. (son of Edmund G. "Pat" Brown Sr.) was elected governor of California, quickly distancing himself from gubernatorial tradition. As the son of a California governor, Brown benefited from name recognition, but his youth and connection to youth culture helped elevate him to the governor's office, along with a wave of newly elected candidates called "the Democratic Class of '74." His predecessor, Ronald Reagan, abandoned the old Governor's Mansion on Fifteenth and H Streets for an East Sacramento home, and Reagan's supporters funded a new mansion in Carmichael. Brown had no interest in the new mansion, comparing its design to a Safeway, and moved into the Dean Apartments across N Street from the state capitol grounds. Instead of mixing with the political elite of the Sutter Club and exclusive political watering holes, Brown preferred casual places like Mexican restaurant 524 in Alkali Flat and dive bars like David's Brass Rail. He exchanged the traditional governor's limousine for a powder-blue Plymouth.

When Brown took office, he rejected a new governor's mansion in the suburbs for the Dean Apartments, across N Street from the capitol. Note commuting cyclist in foreground. *Center for Sacramento History,* Suttertown News *collection.*

Despite Brown's short hair, preference for suits and Jesuit education, he was labeled "California's Hippie Governor" by *People* magazine. His appointments to state commissions reflected a counterculture orientation, including beat hero Gary Snyder to the California Arts Council, later replaced by Peter Coyote, one of the founders of the San Francisco improvisational theater/anarchist group the Diggers. LSD pioneer/author Ken Kesey gave a talk for Brown administration staffers, and Brown granted American Indian Movement (AIM) leader Dennis Banks asylum from extradition to South Dakota. Political activist Tom Hayden served as Brown's research director and consulted with Brown often during his early administration. Brown's attempted appointment of Jane Fonda, at the time Tom Hayden's wife, to the arts council proved too much for the state senate, which blocked the appointment.[10] Brown's invitation was not Hayden's only visit to Sacramento, nor was it Fonda's.

On May 25, 1970, Hayden, then representing Students for a Democratic Society, was prohibited from speaking on the campus of Sacramento State by interim university president Otto Butz. He based this decision on Hayden's status as one of the defendants in the "Chicago Seven" trial and the potential for campus violence, using the precedent of San Jose State's university president, who had blocked a public speech by Chicago Seven defense attorney William Kunstler. Butz may also have hoped to curry favor with Governor Reagan, who had the power to change his "interim" status as University president. On the afternoon of the twenty-sixth, thirty minutes before Hayden was scheduled to speak, U.S. District Court judge Philip C. Wilkins issued a court order overturning Butz's decision. Hayden spoke on the university quad to a crowd of about 150 people, starting thirty minutes late but without demonstrations or disturbances. At an informal gathering outside Douglass Hall with university activists, Hayden said, "Most people still feel the power comes from the silent majority, the power comes from Butz. That's exactly wrong. It's exactly the other way around. [People in official posts were] reacting to the power of youth. After all, they can't get along without the next generation."[11] Later that year, Butz denied a permit to start a gay-interest student club, the Society for Homosexual Freedom, resulting in an October 1970 lawsuit that overturned Butz's refusal. By the time of the decision, Butz had already been replaced as interim president.[12]

In 1975, Tom Hayden ran for U.S. Senate in the Democratic primary, and Jane Fonda traveled to Sacramento to speak to supporters of her husband's campaign at a private fundraiser in Campus Commons on September 12. According to Donald Dean, reporter for the *Suttertown News*,

Jane Fonda addressing Tom Hayden supporters in Sacramento, 1975. *Photo courtesy of Mickey Abbey.*

Mickey Abbey and his friends from the Beginning provided security for Fonda and Hayden on their visits to Sacramento. *Left to right*: Mickey Abbey, Scott Adamson, Steve Ballew, Rick Ball, Rose Lipelt, Richard McCracken, Phil Ballew and Bob Lipelt. *Photo courtesy of Mickey Abbey.*

two groups were represented at the party. A younger contingent in jeans and sandals related to Hayden's earlier radical stance from his Chicago Seven and SDS days. Later in the evening, the party was dominated by "middle-aged/classed/of-the-road" professionals, to whom Hayden had become an acceptable candidate after working with the Brown administration. While in Sacramento, Fonda and Hayden were escorted by a group of artists from the Beginning, the art space/gallery on L Street founded by stained-glass artist Mickey Abbey, metalworker Rick Ball and woodworker Bob Lipelt. The artists' role as security for a counterculture political figure echoed the role played by the Royal Chicano Air Force, which guarded César Chávez when he visited Sacramento. Hayden's U.S. Senate campaign failed by a slim margin, but he later served ten years in the California State Assembly and eight in the state senate.[13]

Tom Hayden's transition from radical outlaw to political candidate mirrored the baby boom generation's moving from radical youth to adulthood. Brown's assumption of power without its residential trappings was derived from the counterculture's rejection of autocentric suburban life.

The young idealists who came to Sacramento hoped to change the system from within, not overthrow it, but maintained many of their counterculture associations of dress, style and association. Many had no interest in their parents' suburban lifestyles, despite their adoption of a professional career in California's bureaucracy. The neighborhoods east of the capitol held great appeal for their proximity to newly consolidating state agencies and for their beautiful architecture and tree-lined sidewalks. As governor of California, Jerry Brown set the example for others to return to the Downtown that his father had helped to vacate.

THE ALIENS OF SACRAMENTO

The term "alien" is used to describe outsiders—generally assumed to be unwelcome or unwanted, with the assumption that they cannot be assimilated

The K Street Mall became a hangout for Sacramento punks in the 1980s. This photo was taken at about Fifth and K Streets; Macy's at Fourth and K is visible in background. *Photo courtesy of Heidi Bennett.*

into mainstream culture—or individuals who challenge the dominant culture through action, artistic expression or thought. The narrative of Sacramento's history often downplays or excludes the alien immigrant in favor of a more Eurocentric model, like the conversion of the West End from a multicultural ethnic neighborhood to a commercial and administrative district, with a designated historic zone dedicated to a valorized age of European settlement. The social alien's evidence in history is difficult to identify, since his characteristics are often internal or psychological and based on his own personal growth, transformation and discovery. Once the alien's presence is revealed, he is often treated as an

24

outcast or pariah, unless he can find other individuals of a common mindset to form a community. In this context, the "alien" includes the bohemian, often unwelcome in suburban settings but flourishing in urban environments.

The Argonauts of the gold rush drew independent thinkers and social misfits and an extraordinarily diverse cultural and racial mix to California, including those who came because they felt outcast from mainstream American life. Once California made its shift from frontier to civilization, the social alien and ethnic alien became equally unwelcome in social discourse. Sacramento, as the seat of state government, took particular pride in its trappings of civilization, growing into an urban, diverse and densely populated city. In the mid-twentieth century, the city's vision of a modern, centerless city resulted in displacement of thirty thousand Downtown residents. The response of those displaced communities to the forces of cultural hegemony became Sacramento's chapter in the American civil rights movement. The civil rights movement inspired young Americans to respond to the dominant culture with counterculture and bohemian expression. This book focuses on Sacramento's cultural and countercultural expressions from the 1960s through the 1980s, not geographically limited to Midtown Sacramento but always returning to the neighborhood on the state capitol's back porch. Midtown is Sacramento's bohemian core, a place to live and a state of mind, and it is the preferred environment of Sacramento's aliens, native and adopted.

"ALIENS IN OUR MIDST" BY THE TWINKEYZ

The stars above us twinkle
Like eyes or flashing teeth
Whose eyes are these that watch us
So many light-years beneath
It seemed so very cold up there
So far from Island Earth
But we've wanted just to join them
From the moment of our birth

Chorus:
There's aliens in our midst
Where they come from, no one knows

There's aliens in our midst
They look like me and you
There's aliens in our midst
This place seems strange to them
There's aliens in our midst
Someday their dreams will come true

This friend of mine was five years old
He dressed up in his sister's clothes
And his daddy got so mad
He whipped him with a rubber hose
But he grew up OK
And made his way to junior high
And as things would have it fell in love
And gave his ring to another guy

Chorus

The rich man and the poor man
The beggar and the thief
They all want money
But can it buy relief?
The workers and the dreamers
They made their bed to lie in
If you pass beneath their windows
Then you might hear them crying

Chorus

1

Where Is Midtown?

If K Street is Sacramento's heart, Midtown is its soul.
—Steve Cohn, Sacramento city council member

The term "Midtown" appeared in the *Sacramento Bee* 31 times in 1984, 138 times in 1990, 367 in 2000 and peaked at 593 mentions in 2010.[14] In *Suttertown News*, a weekly alternative newspaper focused on city life, the term appeared a few times in 1982 and more often in 1983, and by 1984, it was in regular use to promote businesses east of Sixteenth Street. The term emerged as a way to differentiate the old residential, mixed-use neighborhoods from the office districts around the capitol and the increasingly unpopular K Street Mall. This division was also found in early Sacramento history and the outward migration of its middle class.

Early Sacramento was divided into the waterfront West End and the "Homes District" east of Fifth Street. As the city's built environment took form, with the California State Capitol at the city's geographic center, neighborhoods emerged around the K Street business district, following streetcar routes on H, J and K Streets. Growth was constrained by levees on B and R Streets and a drainage ditch on Thirty-first Street. As regional levee networks improved, the R Street levee and drainage system were superseded, promoting growth to the city limits at Y Street until even that street's levee became redundant. Sacramento's original street grid, from the river to Alhambra and B Street to Broadway (the original city limits), were called the "Old City" in the early twentieth century, referring to the original city limits.[15] The term fell from use in the 1980s as "Midtown" became commonplace.

THE HOMES DISTRICT

In 1854, Sacramento's city government created four voting wards based on lines drawn on K and Fifth Streets. West of Fifth Street were the First Ward north of K and the Second Ward to the south. The Third and Fourth Wards, north and south of K Street east of Fifth, ran all the way to the city limits. Half the city's population of about ten thousand lived west of Fifth Street in less than one square mile, while the other half lived in the remaining 80 percent of the city's area.[16] By 1870, Sacramento established its first permanent streetcar line from Front and K Streets, beginning an era of rapid eastward expansion. In 1893, when Sacramento's population neared thirty thousand, a new "Strong Mayor" charter divided the city into nine wards, with wards one through four located along the waterfront, representing thousands of industrial workers and migrant agricultural laborers, mostly living in apartments and rooming houses. The other five districts covered the residential area to Thirty-first Street, primarily single-family homes, thus called the "Homes District." Each ward elected a trustee, but the city was run by an executive mayor. Party politics were an important feature of Sacramento elections, with the West End wards voting Democratic and the Homes District voting Republican. The 1893 charter was followed by a drive to create a chamber of commerce in 1895.

By 1910, the power players on the Democratic Party side were Southern Pacific Railroad, the Buffalo Brewery and suburban real estate mogul Dan Carmichael, supported by thousands of voting migrant workers and immigrants in the West End. Sacramento's Republicans were Progressive political reformers, led in spirit by Teddy Roosevelt and California's new governor, Sacramento-born attorney Hiram Johnson, and locally by real estate developer Clinton L. White and hotelier William Land. Their power base was the middle-class Homes District, whose numbers were also increasing via electric streetcars and new levees. The chamber of commerce's presidents often became mayors of Sacramento, including both Carmichael and White. The Homes District won a victory over Sacramento's industrial managers in 1911 when voters approved a new charter, eliminating the "Strong Mayor" charter with a city commission system and annexing East Sacramento, Oak Park, Curtis Park and Land Park. The charter was revised again in 1921 to a council/manager system, with at-large council members instead of districts, with the council member who received the most votes becoming mayor.[17]

With continued eastward and southward growth, Sacramento's middle class gradually shifted from the Homes District to the new neighborhoods

K Street between Tenth and Eleventh, circa 1920, was the heart of the business district and hub of the city's streetcar network. *Western Railway Museum.*

east of Alhambra Boulevard, as Thirty-first Street was known after the Alhambra Theatre was built in 1927, and south of Broadway, as Y Street was renamed after the Tower Theater was completed in 1938. As wealth moved eastward and southward, traffic, industry and immigrants (all considered equal threats by the Progressives) moved into the Homes District. By the 1930s, a new political order emerged via the chamber of commerce, regulating city hall via at-large council members who lived primarily in

Woolworth's at Tenth and K Streets was a fixture of K Street's retail scene from 1956, when it replaced the Hotel Sacramento, until it closed in 1997. *Photo by Joe Perfecto.*

Land Park or East Sacramento and who almost universally belonged to the Sutter Club. During the Great Depression and Second World War, industrial workers crowded into new apartment buildings and older homes converted to apartments in the Homes District. After the war, plans for redevelopment began and the fate of densely populated, immigrant-dominated Downtown Sacramento was sealed. Between 1950 and 1970, the Old City's population dropped from 58,112 to 27,205.

The cultural shift from middle-class whites to working-class and nonwhite residents in the Homes District reshaped the Old City. The displacement caused by redevelopment resulted in a cultural response by the displaced communities and a dramatic political shift during an era of civil rights struggle. The new stewards of the Old City created their own cultural legacy in the jazz music of the West End, the Chicano muralism of Alkali Flat and Southside Park, the midcentury architecture of Chinatown and Japantown, the clubs and cafés of Lavender Heights and the multitude of languages, foods, religions and traditions embodied in the displaced communities of redevelopment's exodus from the demolished West End. The loss of the West End became a reason to struggle and rebuild and question the ends of redevelopment. The loss of Downtown Sacramento became a catalyst to create a new, de facto cultural district among the shady trees and Victorian architecture of Midtown, an age of renaissance that inspired a new generation to return to the city, a task that would only be possible if there were places for them to live. Without the built environment of the old Homes District, in forms that were simultaneously useful, beautiful, walkable and affordable, this flowering could not have taken place. Midtown could not have emerged on the demolished parking lots or the sterile office buildings of the redeveloped West End. The Sacramento landed elite forgot something every farmer knows. Nothing grows in sterile soil.

NEIGHBORHOODS OF THE OLD CITY

The traditional boundaries of the Old City were the original city limits at Broadway and Alhambra, but the three highways that sliced through the city created new functional boundaries at Third, Twenty-ninth and W

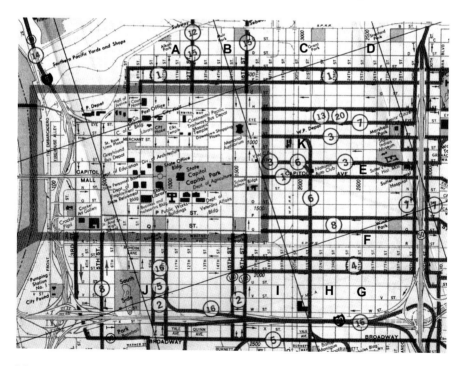

Map of the "Old City," including Downtown and Midtown, lettered by neighborhood, circa 1976. *Author's collection.*

Streets. The gray rectangle on the map on page 31 identifies the boundaries of Sacramento's business district as defined by the Sacramento Transit Authority in 1971, but over time, Midtown crept back into the edges of this zone via rehabilitation and housing construction. In the 1970s, the Old City population reached its lowest ebb. By 2014, most of this business district was far less densely populated than Midtown (not including the Main Jail at Seventh and I Streets), but the neighborhood near Fremont Park at Sixteenth and Q Streets was the most densely populated, with a mixture of new apartments and rehabilitated old buildings. Neighborhood boundaries are fluid and change over time, but the following list identifies some of the Old City's most recognizable neighborhoods.

A is Alkali Flat, the city's oldest-surviving neighborhood, a mixture of 1850s–90s Victorian architecture and 1970s–2010s apartments and urban infill. Proximity to the Southern Pacific Shops made it a working-class neighborhood by 1900, and destruction of the old Sacramento barrio on L Street moved much of the city's Latino population here. Rezoned for commercial development in the 1960s, the Alkali Flat Redevelopment Project Area was established in 1972 to restore housing to the neighborhood, including the 143-unit Washington Square Apartments, *Las Victorianas* senior housing, rehabilitation and relocation of existing homes and development of two new city parks, Zapata Park and J. Neely Johnson Park, between 1973 and 1981.[18]

B is Mansion Flats, previously known as the Washington neighborhood, named for Washington Elementary School. H Street was once known as "Merchant's Row" for its dramatic homes, including the Gallatin and Hale mansions. This neighborhood was home base to the Royal Chicano Air Force, whose first landmarks were the Washington Neighborhood Center on Sixteenth and D Streets, and the La Raza Bookstore Twelfth and F Streets. The name "Mansion Flats" was created by Alicia Wenbourne, who moved to Mansion Flats in 1989. Wenbourne and fellow resident Joe Figueroa formed a neighborhood association to address crime in the neighborhood. The name "Mansion Flats" was inspired by the California Governor's Mansion, located at Sixteenth and H Streets and originally built for Albert Gallatin, designed by Nathaniel Goodell. The Governor's Mansion has been unused as a governor's residence since 1967 but was reopened as a museum.[19] Aside from the mansions along H Street, the neighborhood was largely populated by railroad employees and industrial laborers who could

Dedication of Emiliano Zapata statue at Zapata Park, Alkali Flat. *Center for Sacramento History,* Suttertown News *collection.*

walk to the Southern Pacific shops, canneries and other workplaces along B Street and the Western Pacific Railroad main line between Nineteenth and Twentieth Streets. The area between Sixteenth and Twentieth Streets is still called the Washington neighborhood, referring to the Washington School's contemporary location at Seventeenth and E Streets.

C is Boulevard Park, identifiable by its landscaped, midstreet boulevards along Twenty-first and Twenty-second Streets. From 1861 until 1905, this neighborhood was the site of the Union Park Racetrack, site of the California State Fair's horse and bicycle races and livestock shows. Boulevard Park was a designed landscape, crafted by city engineer William Mulleney and spearheaded by Sacramento attorney, real estate developer and Progressive Republican Clinton L. White. White built his own home in Boulevard Park and became mayor of Sacramento in 1907. White hired the real estate firm of Wright & Kimbrough to sell the properties, either as unimproved lots, made-to-order catalogue homes or speculatively constructed houses of standard design.

Boulevard Park was the first Sacramento residential subdivision to include paved sidewalks, macadamized streets, landscaped street medians, connection to city water and sewer systems and restrictive covenants that mandated building setbacks and design. The most expensive homes on the development's southern end, the H Street streetcar line, included the work of some of Sacramento's best-known architects. Three blocks have parks located in the alleys for use by the adjacent property owners. Lots on Boulevard Park's north end were smaller and affordable to working craftsmen and skilled laborers, with Grant Park along C Street as a public amenity. This was a deliberate decision, intended to provide healthy, beautiful homes for working people. Sales slowed during the depression of 1907, but the neighborhood had developed briskly by 1915 and became one of the city's most coveted addresses. The neighborhood's design elements, including landscaped street medians, blocks reoriented toward the medians and alley parks, make Boulevard Park one of the most cohesive and identifiable Midtown neighborhoods.[20]

D is New Era Park and Marshall School. After the success of Boulevard Park, Wright & Kimbrough developed New Era Park to the east of Boulevard Park, expanding the existing residential neighborhood originally constructed along the H Street streetcar line. Wright & Kimbrough's Craftsman bungalows nestled alongside the Italianate and Queen Anne row houses constructed from the 1870s through the 1890s. Marshall School, named for the elementary school at Twenty-eighth and G Streets, retained a relatively high, 25 percent proportion of homeownership, while overall Old City homeownership dropped to 10 percent by 2010. This percentage was still extremely low compared to Sacramento's overall homeownership percentage of about 59 percent.

The Cranston-Geary mansion at Twenty-first and G Streets, designed by architect George Sellon, is one of Boulevard Park's most prominent Craftsman homes. It was restored by George Bramson. *Photo by author.*

The Western Pacific Railroad passenger depot between J and K Streets. Western Pacific's 1907 arrival in Sacramento broke Southern Pacific's monopoly on long-distance railroads in Sacramento. *Center for Sacramento History.*

E is the neighborhood formally defined as Midtown by the City of Sacramento, between J and R Streets from Fifteenth to Twenty-ninth Streets. Originally the eastern edge of the city, this neighborhood grew in the 1870s via horse-drawn streetcars that ran down K, Twentieth and O Streets. Commercial corridors emerged along electric streetcar lines on J, K, M (renamed Capitol in 1939) and P Streets from the 1890s through the early 1900s. By the 1970s, most of Midtown's streets were converted to one-way couplets intended to speed commuters from highway offramps to Downtown offices and back, with speed limits as high as forty-five miles per hour. Sutter's Fort, including its original central building and the reconstructed outer walls, is located in this part of the city, marking the oldest building in Sacramento and its first historic landmark. The term "Midtown" was probably first used to describe the business district along J, K and L Streets.

F is R Street, the line of Sacramento Valley Railroad, California's first steam railroad, completed in 1856. Originally raised on a levee, R Street was Sacramento's de facto southern border until 1902, when the levee was moved south to Y Street. Railroad-served industries emerged along R Street in the 1850s, but the 1902 levee removal spurred new industrial growth. A second railroad line along Whitney Avenue, between Q and R Streets, was constructed by competitor Western Pacific Railroad in 1907–10, bringing more industrial development to R Street. The corridor was a major job center until railroad business declined in the 1960s. In the 1970s and 1980s, some of the vacant industrial buildings along this corridor became art studios, galleries and businesses, including the Fox & Goose Restaurant, Art Foundry, Stucco Factory and R Street Complex.

G is Newton Booth, named after the elementary school at Twenty-seventh and V Streets, the last corner of the Old City to be developed. Prior to 1902 there were several small dairy farms and orchards in this neighborhood. Streetcar lines along Twenty-eighth Street promoted growth at its eastern end. In 1908, a streetcar line from Southside Park to Twenty-eighth and T Streets spurred construction of bungalows and apartments, filling the neighborhood with homes.

H is Poverty Ridge, Midtown's only hill. The name derives from stories claiming that poorer residents of early Sacramento rushed up this hill to escape floods. By the end of the century, Poverty Ridge was served by a streetcar line on Twenty-first Street and was becoming a highly desirable

This corner store at Fifteenth and Q Streets, formerly the Real Food Company, suffered a fire in the late 1990s and was restored into a coffee shop and apartment building by joint efforts between CADA and SOCA members. *Photo by Joe Perfecto.*

The Roan House at Twenty-second and T Streets in Poverty Ridge, designed by Seadler & Hoen. Joan Didion lived here with her stepgrandmother Genevieve Didion while attending McClatchy High School. *Photo by author.*

The Buffalo Club at Nineteenth and S Streets, formerly the taproom for the Buffalo Brewery, had become a lesbian bar by the late 1970s. *Center for Sacramento History,* Suttertown News *collection.*

address, with some of the city's wealthiest families building homes here to enjoy the view of the Capitol and relative immunity from floods. A short-lived attempt to rebrand the neighborhood "Sutter's Terrace" in the early 1900s did not succeed. Joan Didion lived in Poverty Ridge, briefly as a child at Twenty-second and U Street and later at her aunt's house at Twenty-second and T Streets, so she could attend McClatchy High School.

I is Richmond Grove, originally a park at Twentieth and Q Streets, demolished when Western Pacific Railroad ran through Midtown in 1907–10. Like R Street, the corridor between Nineteenth and Twentieth had many industrial customers, providing employment for those who lived nearby. North of R Street between Roosevelt Park on Tenth and Fremont Park on Sixteenth, entire blocks were demolished for the State Capitol Plan, an enormous office complex envisioned by Edmund G. "Pat" Brown, with one residence, a new governor's mansion, at its center. The plan was shelved by his successor, Governor Ronald Reagan, but clearance of blocks continued to provide parking for state employees. When Jerry Brown took office in 1974, he appointed architect Sim van der Ryn to reimagine the state-owned blocks as the Capitol Area Plan, a mixed-use neighborhood closely resembling the neighborhood they had just demolished, in function if not in form.

Tony López, Southside Park native and neighborhood activist. Tony was involved with efforts to develop R Street as a mixed-use corridor instead of an office district. *Center for Sacramento History,* Suttertown News *collection.*

In 1978, Capitol Area Development Authority, a joint-powers authority, was created to administer this area. It supervised construction of new state office buildings, but it also restored much of the housing demolished and created more housing where needed. CADA relocated old single-family homes from out of the path of demolition, and built new apartments. As a result, the end of the neighborhood north of R Street was restored to a higher population density than any other part of the Old City by 2010 but was still only 60 percent of its 1950 population.[21]

J is Southside Park, the Old City's most diverse neighborhood. Originally settled by Irish, Portuguese and Italian immigrants, the population of Southside organized to advocate for improvements, including removal of an incinerator on Front Street that rained ash on the neighborhood after little Daisy Dias perished after falling into the hot ash pile behind the incinerator in 1915. The Southsiders also advocated for removal of the R Street levee, urged Pacific Gas & Electric to run a streetcar line down T Street and convinced the City of Sacramento to build a major park between Sixth and Eighth Streets on the site of an old slough. During the redevelopment era, the Italian and Portuguese communities relocated to East Sacramento and Land Park, as more Chinese and Japanese moved into Southside.

Patrons of the Wreck Room, 920 Twentieth Street, in Lavender Heights. *Photo courtesy Lavender Library and Cultural Exchange.*

Sacramento's Latino community also had a strong presence in Southside, represented by the Mexican Center on Sixth and W Streets and Our Lady of Guadalupe Church on Eighth and T. Southside Park was an important site for the diverse neighborhood's cultural celebrations, so the RCAF utilized the park for public events. Southside Park is also home to California's oldest Muslim mosque, located on Fourth and U Streets. This neighborhood was closely connected to Sacramento's waterfront, including the heavy industrial district along Front Street, severed by Interstate 5 in the late 1960s. Interstate 5, Highway 50 and Capitol Mall isolated Southside Park from surrounding neighborhoods on three sides. The neighborhood's tradition of activism never abated, and in the early 1980s, groups formed to chase prostitution out of Southside by picketing the notorious prostitutes' crawl at Fourth and T Streets.[22]

K is Lavender Heights. In 1998, Chico State University geography student Michael Clausen described the geography of an emerging gay and lesbian community in Sacramento, including the results of a survey of neighborhood residents. While few agreed where the outer edges of Lavender Heights were, almost all agreed that the neighborhood's center was Twentieth and K Streets. Within two blocks along Twentieth Street are a row of bars, including the Wreck Room, the Western (now the Depot), Christie's Elbo Room (now Faces), Club 21 and the Mercantile. Bars and nightlife are only one aspect of the Lavender Heights community, but they are the most visible. This visibility is of particular importance. Prior to the 1970s, gay bars were secretive and private, due to fear of public exposure and the very real risk of arrest and imprisonment. Gay liberation allowed the gay community to emerge from the shadows, creating a social atmosphere that fostered diversity. Sacramento's Lambda Center, a social service and support organization, opened at Twentieth and L Streets in 1986.

The Lambda Center was funded in part by a lawsuit against Reverend Jerry Falwell brought forth by Sacramento Metropolitan Community Church (MCC) founder Gerry Sloane. Sloane and Falwell were friends and classmates at Baptist Bible College in Springfield, Missouri. After graduation, Falwell became a national figure for the Religious Right, founder of the Moral Majority political action committee. Sloane came out as gay and founded chapters of the MCC in Kansas City, Des Moines and Sacramento. Sloane remained interested in Falwell's career and watched his television program. On March 11, 1984, he was shocked to hear Falwell describe MCC as an embodiment of evil, ending with, "Thank God this vile

The 1981 Sacramento Gay Pride Parade, near Fremont Park. By the early 1980s, Lavender Heights had developed its own political action committees and endorsed local political races. *Lavender Library And Cultural Exchange.*

and satanic system will one day be utterly annihilated, and there will be a celebration in heaven."

When both were guests on a Sacramento television show five months later, Sloane challenged Falwell about his statements, but Falwell denied saying them, offering $5,000 if Sloane could provide a tape proving him wrong. Sloane produced the tape, but Falwell claimed that the quote was inaccurate, as Sloane claimed he used the word "rejoicing," not "celebration." Sloane won the judgment in September 1985, and despite Falwell's efforts to overturn the decision, he paid $8,982 to Sloane. After attorney's fees were paid, Sloan used the balance to buy furniture and office equipment for the fledgling Lambda Center. In return for Falwell's involuntary contribution, Sloane named a closet in the Lambda Center in Falwell's honor.[23]

GOVERNING MIDTOWN

In 1970, Sacramento voters approved a charter change as dramatic as the shift from "Strong Mayor" in 1911 to the mayor-council system in 1920. Instead of at-large city council members, elected citywide, the city was divided into eight districts, each with a single council member. The charter change was a product of the civil rights movement, with groups like the League of Women Voters advocating for the change. Anne Rudin, who grew up in Philadelphia and moved to Sacramento from Riverside in 1958, was a League of Women Voters board member during this era. The league advocated for the change based on the lack of representation in Sacramento's poorer neighborhoods. With the charter change, Rudin was persuaded to run for a city council seat.[24]

I think the League persuaded the mayor to establish a new committee to vote for our council members by district, and a separate election for mayor. Until then, you just had a general election and the nine highest vote getters became the city council, and the one among them, the highest of the nine, got to be mayor. We found that all the council members were coming from…where

Mayor Anne Rudin responding to the *Old City Guardian*, Sacramento Old City Association's newsletter and neighborhood newspaper, circa 1989. *Photo by Joe Perfecto.*

more rich people lived. They were coming from East Sacramento, there were very few council members coming from North Sacramento, which was mostly [a] minority [neighborhood] but part of the city. We decided that we wanted to have district elections. The council put it on the ballot, and I think it failed the first time it was on the ballot, there was another election and then it passed. I believe that was when I was persuaded to run for the city council. I didn't really want to have all that responsibility…I was persuaded by Citizens for Better Government, a local group. I was a member of it; we had all worked to get the district system installed here in Sacramento. Several of them persuaded me to run. They hadn't had a woman elected to the City Council since Belle Cooledge.

—Anne Rudin

Phil Isenberg was born in Erie, Indiana, but grew up in Sacramento. He graduated from Sacramento State in 1961 before studying law at Berkeley and worked for the state senate and legislature before entering local politics. Prior to running for city council, he ran for the state Democratic Central Committee and was beaten by Royal Chicano Air Force member Joe Serna. Isenberg and Serna became close friends after the election.

You had to run citywide, and to run citywide you have to have a really substantial campaign. The rap on the city of Sacramento was, Downtown businesses dominated city council, and mayor was elected by the council members. So '71 was the first [directly] elected mayor, and I think all eight seats for the council were up at that time…it was the only way I was going to be elected! I can't remember—we may have spent $3,000 on the campaign, maybe. You know, Maurice [Reid] and his then partner Audrey Tsuruda did the campaign for free. We hand-painted the signs. A lot of the posters were done at Joe Serna's garage by the guys who were known as the RCAF, Royal Chicano Air Force.

—Phil Isenberg

The 1971 election was the first in over sixty years with a directly elected mayor. The candidates were both previous at-large council members Richard Marriott, mayor prior to the charter change, and Milton McGhee, at the time Sacramento's only black city council member. Marriott won the mayoral election. Manuel Ferrales, Sacramento's first Latino council member (elected in 1969) and founder of the Sacramento Concilio social service organization, retained his seat on the council. Most of the 1971

Phil Isenberg served as a city council member and mayor of Sacramento before serving in the California State Assembly and Senate. *Center for Sacramento History, Suttertown News collection.*

Council member Robert Matsui, Sacramento's first Japanese American council member, later served in the U.S. House of Representatives. *Center for Sacramento History, Suttertown News collection.*

council members were new to the council, including R. Burnett Miller, Anne Rudin, Phil Isenberg, Rosenwald "Robbie" Robertson (a black minister from Del Paso Heights) and Robert Matsui (Sacramento's first Japanese American council member.) For many of Sacramento's old guard and business community, the new council represented a grave threat to their traditional authority over city government.[25]

> *When we got elected in 1971, Bruce Allen was a partner in the McDonough, Schwartz & Allen law firm...Bruce got quoted, "The red flag of rebellion has gone up over city hall!" It was hysterical; it was just a hoot. For guys who had run the city, it was a big deal. Later, the* [older members of the] *chamber of commerce, and it was mostly a chamber of a few old anti-young-people, wanted to make peace, so they decided to hold a reception for the newly elected council members at the Sutter Club, where I had never been. And I think it was the day before the reception, they called over to city hall, somewhat embarrassed to say that they wanted to go on with the reception, but Anne can't come, because* [they] *didn't let women into the Sutter Club! And that was just great because we were able to boycott the meeting and make mean statements about the Sutter Club, and they looked like fucking idiots—as they were! And we didn't have to go to the Sutter Club for years after that...At the time, they felt it was a striking change.*
> —Phil Isenberg

REDISTRICTING SPLITS THE OLD CITY

District elections divided the Old City between District 1, North Sacramento and Natomas, represented by Manuel Ferrales, and District 4, Land Park, represented by Anne Rudin. Marshall School was placed in District 3, represented by Burnett Miller. Division into three council districts meant that no single council member directly represented the entire Old City, and each was also responsible for a much larger outlying neighborhood. This had advantages, including three potential votes to support projects that might not receive support from outlying districts, but no council member had a specific Downtown focus. Neighborhoods within the Old City had difficulty collaborating as a single larger neighborhood because they were located in different districts. Often, Downtown policy was driven by the mayor, the only at-large council position, but only if the mayor held a particular interest in Downtown.

Above: Children enjoyed the water features of K Street's geometric concrete sculptures, but they were not well regarded by most Sacramentans. *Photo by Joe Perfecto.*

Left: Sacramento transit activist Wayne Hultgren crusaded for better public transit, including bringing light rail to K Street. *Center for Sacramento History,* Suttertown News *collection.*

In 1975, Phil Isenberg ran to replace Richard Marriott as mayor. During the 1975 election season, Isenberg was differentiated from his challenger, David McKinley, considered the business candidate. Isenberg believed that Downtown Sacramento was entering a new period of growth, due to rising fuel costs and disillusionment with suburban living. He also saw a connection between this return to the city and the environmental movement. McKinley felt the suburban way of life was too compelling for people to give up and was more interested in new suburban subdivisions than reshaping Downtown Sacramento, pointing at the underperforming K Street Mall and Convention Center as proof that Downtown investment did not work. Sacramento voters backed Isenberg, reaffirming Isenberg's direction on Downtown development.[26]

Every decade, Sacramento's city council districts were reapportioned. Community groups and organizations submitted proposed boundaries based on equal population, equal representation, compactness and contiguity, communities of interest and political boundary integrity. Sacramento's highly integrated neighborhoods and overlapping constituencies meant that redistricting was complex, with different communities competing for representation. In 1981, the city provided redistricting kits with maps, statistical information and blank forms for interested parties. The 1980 census data indicated an increase of about three thousand people in the Old City, but the most dramatic citywide shift was growth in the black community, especially the Meadowview neighborhood, divided into two districts by the 1971 district map. The Sacramento Area Black Caucus submitted a map uniting the Meadowview neighborhood, but shortly before the deadline, council member Thomas Chinn submitted another map that divided Meadowview in half and divided the Old City differently.

Instead of the southeast/northwest division between Districts 1 and 4, the Old City was divided north and south along R Street. This put the central business district and the northern half of Midtown in the same district. From 1981 to 1989, David Shore served as the District 1 council member. Shore lived in Boulevard Park and was acutely aware of neighborhood issues. Newton Booth and Poverty Ridge joined Southside Park in the more residentially oriented District 4. District 3 retained its small corner, dominated by East Sacramento. Also in 1981, Joe Serna was elected to serve District 5 after years of experience working with community groups and on local political campaigns.

After Phil Isenberg was elected to the California State Assembly in 1982, he was briefly replaced by Burnett Miller as mayor. Anne Rudin won the

Above: Gay pride parade at Tenth and L Streets. *Photo by Joe Perfecto.*

Left: Capitol Mall, circa 1960. Redevelopment created a grand architectural entrance to Sacramento but destroyed the residential neighborhoods of the West End that gave downtown Sacramento its cultural and economic vitality. *Center for Sacramento History.*

1983 mayoral election, becoming the first directly elected female mayor of Sacramento. Rudin courted voters in Midtown, including the gay community in Lavender Heights, and members of Downtown neighborhood groups including the Sacramento Old City Association.[27]

In 1991, the River City Democratic Club (RCDC), a gay/lesbian organization, tried to unite Sacramento's central city into a single city council district, consolidating the parts of the city most associated with Lavender Heights into District 3, spreading east into East Sacramento. At the time of the 1991 redistricting effort, the gay community lacked equal representation in this area, but the RCDC plan proposed a newly unified central city district to achieve that end.

Six groups submitted their own redistricting maps, including one created by a coalition of the Latino Coalitions for Fair Sacramento Redistricting and the Summit on African American Concerns. Their coalition map split Sacramento's central city into three districts, leaving the gay community with substantially less political influence and dividing central city neighborhoods into adjacent districts. District 3 was extended to Twenty-first Street, and District 1 and 4 were divided along Capitol Avenue. This boundary split created problems for the Lambda Community Center, the political heart of Lavender Heights, by separating its office at Twentieth and L Streets from much of the nearby LGBT population in the southern half of Midtown and the Downtown neighborhoods of Alkali Flat and Mansion Flats. The coalition plan was adopted, widening the rift between Downtown and Midtown, but by 1990, Midtown had already asserted its own countercultural identity, beginning in the 1960s and 1970s.[28]

2

Big John Versus the Teenage Rock-and-Roll Aliens

The earliest hip place I can remember was the Eye on Fourteenth and K, I think, across the street from Capitol Chevrolet. It was psychedelic clothes, incense, one of the first head shops to open up in town, in '67. The first hip bar was where the hospital is now…Twenty-ninth and L. I think this bar was called the Public House Tavern. Good old feel, lot of wood, all the old-timers, and you'd see young cats drinking, too. That was the first place we could gather. Randy Paragary opened the Parapow Palace on Thirtieth and O, and I know that it cost him $900 to open the place, and he made it back the first week. Randy has gone on to do much. I went in there with Alice Cooper once for an after-show party, sat there and drank beer with Alice. I tell you, I went to every fuckin' show at the [Memorial] Auditorium. First shows by the Kinks, the Dave Clark Five, the Rolling Stones. I was a big Who fan, and on their first American tour, they opened up for Herman's Hermits. There were two shows, 3:00 and 7:00 [p.m.]. The audience is three thousand ten-year-old girls and their mothers and six teenage boys! So the Who comes out, they play twenty minutes, they smash their equipment, set off smoke bombs, total carnage, and walk off the stage. We were going, "Yeah, yeah!" and three thousand teenage girls and their moms were sitting there with their mouths open, waiting for "Henry the Eighth I am!" And they did it again for the second show.
—Jeff Hughson

Known as "Big John," John Misterly was sheriff of Sacramento County from 1961 until 1971. Misterly's law enforcement style focused on stemming the cultural tide of the 1960s from reaching Sacramento

County. His efforts included infiltration of antiwar groups at CSUS and a successful bid to prohibit comedian Lenny Bruce from performing in Sacramento, especially ironic as Misterly had a reputation for profanity. With an appearance like a cigar-chomping bulldog, he became a caricature of police oppression to a generation of Sacramento youth. Misterly's policies also influenced Sacramento's city police department, setting a tone of conflict between young, creative people and law enforcement.

Sheriff John "Big John" Misterly. *Center for Sacramento History,* Sacramento Bee *Collection.*

Born in Springfield, Massachusetts, in 1912, Misterly came to California in 1932, hoping to join the Olympic pistol team. Failing to make the team, he found work at a San Francisco biscuit company, moving in 1935 to Santa Rosa, where he became a part-time special investigator for the Sonoma County Sheriff's Department, run by his wife's cousin Tom Money. He joined the state police in 1939, working on Angel Island and then transferred to the California Highway Patrol in 1941, specializing in narcotics enforcement. He moved to Sacramento in 1947, supervising antidrug efforts throughout northern California until he was appointed sheriff in 1961 by the Sacramento County Board of Supervisors.[29]

Misterly's predecessor, Don Cox, oversaw the Sheriff's Department from 1932 until retiring due to ill health in 1961. During those twenty-nine years, Sacramento County grew from a rural region, whose unincorporated population was less than half that of the City of Sacramento, to a largely urbanized county where 60 percent of its 503,000 residents lived outside the city limits. Deputies often worked out of their homes, one deputy per 2,400 residents, or as the Sacramento Union described it, "spread as thin as the butter on a boardinghouse roll." Misterly used his experience working for state law enforcement agencies to modernize his department and petition the county board of supervisors for more funds.

In May 1961, an article in the *Sacramento Union* described a meeting of the Sacramento Moslem League, a local black Muslim group, featuring speaker Malcom X on what may have been his only visit to Sacramento. Local leader Anwar Ali Khan denounced Misterly's policies, described as persecution of black Muslims in Sacramento. One of the speakers at the May 1961 event, Bernard Moore (aka Bernard X) was subsequently arrested and institutionalized for draft evasion. Moore appealed his charges, claiming the arrest was motivated by his public criticism of Misterly.[30]

Another special target of Misterly's attention was the Hell's Angels motorcycle gang. His efforts were mentioned in Hunter S. Thompson's book *Hell's Angels*, which described Misterly's efforts as extreme enough to chase the Angels entirely from Sacramento by 1965. The sole exception to Misterly's war on the Angels was a one-day truce in January 1966 for the funeral of James T. "Mother" Miles, leader of the Sacramento chapter. Two to three hundred Angels converged on the Nicoletti Funeral Home in a solemn but loud procession, punctuated by the roar of motorcycles, to East Lawn Cemetery less than a mile away. Representatives of eleven chapters of the Hell's Angels from throughout California paid their respects and then left Sacramento with a police escort following close behind, eager to ensure their departure. Sheriff Misterly could not abide a Hell's Angels wake within the borders of Sacramento County.[31]

Not every target of Misterly's ire was as obvious as the Hell's Angels. In 1968, he tried to shut down the Kairos Coffee House, a café run by the Carmichael United Church of Christ on El Camino Avenue. Misterly wanted the café closed down "long enough to get rid of that bunch of hippies with pockets stuffed with marijuana they're attracting. Membership should be limited to church members and their guests—not a wide-open spot for every misfit in the county." The coffeehouse, started by Reverend Rod MacKenzie, was intended as a gathering place for student communication, poetry readings and folk music. MacKenzie resisted Misterly's efforts more successfully than the Hell's Angels. Several drug arrests near the coffeehouse drew negative media attention, but one of the purposes of Kairos was to provide an alternative for young people to the drug scene. A young leader of the coffeehouse, Andrew Morin, described Kairos as "the only tie-in with adults who care."[32]

Funeral for Sacramento Hell's Angels chapter president, "Mother" Miles, on Folsom Boulevard, 1965. *Center for Sacramento History,* Sacramento Bee *Collection.*

According to a series of *Sacramento Union* articles recounting Misterly's legacy in May 1970, shortly before his final election campaign, his key accomplishments included a low crime rate and efforts to keep the mafia, Hell's Angels, narcotics and gambling out of Sacramento County. Misterly also targeted hippies, specifically rock music festivals, and teen centers he considered inappropriately run, including Kairos. In his own words, "Now, I've always supported the community youth centers…But when you come to a commercial teenage nightclub concept, the coffeeshop concept…I'm against it."[33] The *Union* gave Misterly's campaign considerable space during the end of May 1970, including a profile of his anti-vice campaign. A May 28 letter to the editor from Dorothy Weber commended Misterly for keeping rock festivals out of Sacramento and suppressing public protests: "Misterly harasses hop-heads constantly. I like that! If the younger generation is against Misterly, it's because they insist on breaking the law and can't stand the one man who insists on trying to enforce it."

Union editor Tom Horton also penned an editorial on city pride, recounting the tale of a fictional old woman who wanted to see Sacramento recognized as a major city, pleased by evidence of urban growth and irritated by those who called Sacramento a cow town. She realized the folly of her ways reading an article about a group of elementary students in Burney, a small town in northern California, who decided against a school trip to Sacramento because of "urban unrest." The killing of Officer Bernard Bennett by a sniper in Oak Park on May 2, 1970, the event that precipitated the Oak Park Four murder trial, justified the little Shasta County school's cancellation of a trip to the state capital. The years of racial conflict in Oak Park were preceded by displacement of populations through redevelopment, but the fear of those schoolchildren was enough to convince her to give up her dreams of an urban Sacramento and instead wish for her hometown to become a less interesting place.[34]

THE ANCIL HOFFMAN PARK RIOT

On March 15, 1970, Misterly coordinated a raid on Ancil Hoffman Park, an event that some Sacramentans felt was timed for maximum effect on voters, securing his reputation as a "law and order" candidate in an era of social unrest. The incident apparently displeased potential voters upset by the incident and Misterly's heavy-handed style. Despite the accolades of the *Union*, Misterly lost his 1970 reelection bid. Ancil Hoffman Park includes nearly four hundred acres alongside the American River, including nature trails and a golf course. By 1970, it was a preferred hangout of young people, including high school and college students. The privacy and natural setting of the park made it a popular spot for marijuana users and thus a target for law enforcement activity. On the day of the raid, about sixty Sheriff's deputies, including forty in riot gear, formed a skirmish line at one end of the park at about 1:30 p.m., backed up by twenty-two California Highway Patrol officers. At about 3:00 p.m., undercover officers approached an estimated two to three hundred young people in the park and began arresting those who were smoking marijuana.

Sheriff Misterly had been staking out the park with deputies on the Rancho [Cordova] side with binoculars for some days. The reason there were photos so early on in the incident is because he alerted the newspapers ahead of time so they could write it up. After the cops rounded up the kids smoking weed on the riverbank and put them in patrol cars, a plainclothes officer started dragging this kid around who was pretty messed up on something, probably reds. A bunch of kids saw how he was treating this incapacitated kid and, not knowing he was a cop, started getting in his face. He then identified himself. Then the kids saw that he was unarmed [and] started surrounding and harassing him. That's when he called for backup, and the whole department was there. It was pretty funny watching all the officers pull out their new riot gear and exchanging items, trying to get the gear on etc. They then swept the park with a baton-to-baton sweep and forced everyone out of the park. "Leave the park or you will be arrested" was their chant. So we did, very gradually. This took hours. But along the way, they grabbed anyone who didn't move fast enough and treated them pretty poorly for no real good reason other than they could. Remember, they had their new riot gear on. So I made my way out of the park via the nature area and parked outside the park thinking I wouldn't be caught up [in] the ruckus, even though I was part of it. My girlfriend all along kept saying, "Let's just go," but no, I was a revolutionary! After a few interactions with the deputies outside the park (where they [had] asked us to go) I decided it was time to go home for my birthday dinner. Boy, how I had worked up an appetite!

As I was getting in my car I saw a group of officers point toward me so I got in and locked my door. Ha! Like that helped. A big arm came through my wing window, opened the door and dragged me out. They told me I was under arrest for assaulting a police officer with a deadly weapon and asked, "How old are you, punk?" and I said, "I turned eighteen today!" He said, "Then you're going to jail, not juvie." About that time I realized how stupid I was. My parents let me stew overnight in the felony ward where I was a bit of a celebrity because, to these guys, I tried to kill a cop. The next morning, my dad picked me up and marched me over to the post office, where I had to register for the draft—not that my dad thought it was a good idea, because he would have rather sent us to Canada then go fight in Vietnam, but because it was nearby and the law. But it sure got my attention for the twelfth time in twenty-four hours. We got in his car, and there were the Sac Bee and Union on the car seat with the articles. He took me for burgers and gave me some facts of life, and there, my friends, is probably why I'm still here today. Not that I never made trouble, I just never got caught again. I turned out OK. And by the way, it was just pot smoking that started the whole thing and the fact that Sheriff Misterly was up for reelection. He didn't succeed.

—Tom Borgsdorf [35]

Police in riot gear prepare to remove young people from a grassy hill at Cal Expo on August 24, 1971. The resulting riot ended with sixteen arrests. *Center for Sacramento History, Sacramento Bee Collection.*

The young man mentioned above as "messed up on something" was sixteen-year-old Clayton McCormach, visiting from Pleasant Hill. Officers attempted to subdue him, but he resisted and was restrained. Other members of the crowd became angry for what they viewed as unjust, excessive force. They pelted the police with bottles, cans and stones and overturned a detective's police car. The police skirmish line moved in and became more aggressive with arrests in an effort to clear the park. Thirty-five people were arrested for marijuana possession and other charges related to the riot. Members of the Delta Sigma Pi fraternity, holding a pledge picnic at the park, assisted the police, as Misterly described: "They went to the aid of the officers and helped to prevent more serious damage." By 4:30 p.m., the park was cleared except for golfers on the park's golf course, who played, uninterrupted, through the riot.[36]

I just remembered him being an unbelievable redneck, he was basically anti-hippie and anything that had anything to do with that. As far as Sacramento County getting a good bang for their buck from a sheriff, as far

57

as taking care of crime in general, I don't think he was worth a damn. But I was out there at Ancil Hoffman Park when they did the infamous raid. I think they arrested a few dozen people and most everybody else just melted into the woods and didn't get arrested. It was quite a scene...I think it kind of cooled things down, but it didn't stop anything. It's not like Misterly had a defined plan or an overall vision of what the hell he was trying to do; he was just kind of a reactionary old fart with old-school ideas.

—David Rolin

MOVING THE SACRAMENTO CRUISE

One reason for K Street's conversion into a pedestrian mall, in addition to attracting suburban shoppers Downtown, was removal of the legendary K Street cruise. John Misterly and other Sacramento authorities viewed late-night gatherings of youth as potential threats. According to Phil Isenberg, who grew up in Sacramento during the era of the cruise: "In high school, we used to come down to cruise K Street, drive around with the windows down looking for girls, mostly unsuccessfully. The cruise was the place to go, a lot more exciting than the mall is most of the time these days." Sacramento had a rich tradition of custom cars, starting in the 1930s and growing through the 1960s. Contemporary accounts of the K Street cruise compare it to a scene out of *American Graffiti,* the classic George Lucas movie filmed in Modesto. Sacramento's hot rod scene and cruise was larger and far more ethnically diverse.

K Street was one way going down the river and then you had your choice between coming back up J or coming back up L, depending on which one you wanted to hit. Nineteenth and J was a popular destination or cruise through, which was Mel's Drive In, and if you wanted to hang out and see the better cars on a Friday or Saturday night, Mel's Drive In was a good place to be. There was, at Sixteenth and L, a Firestone tire dealership that had one of those diagonal parking lots in front of it...in the evening it was just an off-street place to park, and that's where you could go to find a race if you were looking to get some money or pink slips if that's what you wanted to do. People with the hotter cars would be hanging around there, and they'd go out to El Centro Road. I don't know how long it was, but miles of two-lane country road with no cross roads...a good place to go street racing. You could go out there, put on the slicks, unplug the headers, get all the weight out of the trunk and race until you got tired of it.

—David Rolin

David Rolin was born in Whittier, California, in 1938. He grew up in a military family, and in 1948, his father was transferred from a base in Japan to McClellan Air Force Base. The family celebrated Christmas on the high seas before arriving in Sacramento for David's father's three-year assignment. David's parents were both automobile enthusiasts, and cars were a large part of David's childhood. He built his first custom car in 1954, before he even had a driver's license, and in 1957, he gave up an appointment to West Point to return to Sacramento and be part of the custom car scene. He got married in Sacramento and moved to Curtis Park. As a wedding gift, his father made a down payment on a 1957 Ford Fairlane. David used the skills he learned from his family and the hot rod community to turn the brand-new car into a work of art, known as the Tormentor:

I bought it and removed all the chrome from the outside, filled the hood, trunk, door handles. And then went to the drags one day, was trying to get a set of slicks that could fit on the back, and I couldn't. So I took a torch and hot-wrenched the wheel well and the back fenders, continued by day racing. I took it to Tognotti's body shop, and they finished off the wheel wells properly, basically cleaned up the damage I did, and rolled the rear pan. That was about it for that stage. At that point, I had some minor engine work, three-twos on it, headers and ignition. I think it was kind of a work in progress. It was my daily driver so I'd work on it and drive it, work on it and drive it.

David cruised K Street and raced on the weekends, but during the week he attended American River College (ARC), studying industrial design, planning a move to Los Angeles to become an automobile designer. While attending ARC, his art instructors noted David's creative talent. One told him, "You don't want to wind up designing hubcaps the rest of your life— you're a good artist!" David took their advice and transferred to Sacramento State, pursuing a degree in fine art. He also reevaluated his life within the context of the changing social times of the 1960s and became more aware of the antiwar movement. He turned his back on hot rodding for many years, discovering an affinity for jewelry and fine art, and became involved in the local music scene as road manager for local band the New Breed. From

Above: David Rolin's "Tormentor" was a regular on the K Street cruise until David abandoned the hot rod scene to become a jeweler and fine artist. *Courtesy of David Rolin.*

Left: Parade grand marshal Stan Lemkuil atop his Studebaker, Old Sacramento, July 3, 1980. *Photo by Joe Perfecto.*

graduation until 1973, he was an art teacher at a grade school in North Sacramento, where he shared his counterculture values with his students. One day, a little girl asked him, "Mr. Rolin, why do you still drive a car and live in a regular house?" This statement, made innocently enough by a child, again made David reassess his life, and he moved his family to a dome tent in rural Oregon later in 1973, where he pursued a living as a full-time jeweler and artist.[37]

The closure of K Street in 1969 did not end the Sacramento cruise; drivers simply rerouted to J and L Streets around the mall. The rise of the Chicano movement brought another generation's mechanical artistry, the lowrider, to the already multicultural Sacramento cruise. Emerging first in Southern California, lowrider clubs quickly became part of the Sacramento hot rod scene. In 1978, the presence of lowriders in a slow orbit around the K Street Mall provoked outrage from John Kehoe, vice-president of the chamber of commerce, who outlined the threat at a Downtown merchants' brunch: "People came into the chamber [offices] seeking refuge because these teenage gangs were marauding. These boys have balloon pants, and in the pants [they have] pipes and knives. They love to terrorize senior citizens." The *Sacramento Bee* and *Union* responded with outraged articles, leading to a forcible southward shift of the cruise to Broadway and Franklin Boulevard.

The cruise continued in its new location but resulted in a high-profile incident. In October 1979, two policemen attempted to arrest two boys in the parking lot of the Farmer's Market supermarket on Broadway and Franklin for outstanding traffic violations. The boys (and three girls traveling with them) resisted, and the police maced and beat them. The lowriders claimed the attack was unprovoked, and they became known as the "Franklin Five." The parents of one of the girls sued the city for violation of civil rights, assault and battery and false imprisonment. Thirty residents of Southside Park formed the Parent Patrol, which kept watch on the cruise to protect the lowriders' civil rights. Members of the Royal Chicano Air Force and La Raza Lawyers' Association also came to the lowriders' defense. Members of the Sacramento City Council, including Anne Rudin and Lloyd Connelly, and merchants' associations along Franklin Boulevard brought pressure on police to curtail the cruise in the name of public safety. In March 1980, Mayor Phil Isenberg accepted an invitation to cruise the boulevard in a symbolic gesture to find a middle ground, and later that year, the "Franklin Five" case was resolved, with one youth pleading guilty to resisting arrest and the other four receiving an out-of-court settlement.[38]

THE "PINK PUSSY KAT A GO-GO" TRIAL

In the summer of 1969, Sheriff Misterly arrested two dancers at an Orangevale strip club, Suzanne Haines and Sheila Brendenson, for indecent exposure and the bar's owner, Leonard L. Glancy, for soliciting the dancers to perform a lewd act. This bust was part of Misterly's efforts to curtail vice in Sacramento County, but it became a battle over free expression and the female form, presided over by the son of a former California governor and Supreme Court Chief Justice.

> *I remember going to the Alameda Burlesque in high school, where the famous show was* Tassel Time at the Alameda. *We were all underage, but we were drinking purloined alcohol from our parents…it was an old burlesque theater. One of the dancers had tassels on her nipples, and her skill was to make them go in opposite directions. When you're drunk and a teenager, that's a big scene!*
>
> —Phil Isenberg

By the late 1960s, burlesque and strip clubs were forced out of Downtown Sacramento by a combination of redevelopment and regulation. Redevelopment demolished many of the small theaters that became burlesque halls in the 1950s, like the Alameda and New Star, to make way for office complexes and the Downtown Plaza. The New Rio's efforts to revive burlesque in 1965 were stifled by a local code allowing the city assessor to deny a business license based on a threat to public morals.[39] Another burlesque theater, the Roxie at 912 Ninth Street, was demolished during the same era. The Roxie was first built as the Plaza Theater in 1927. By 1949, the Roxie featured lurid after-midnight shows, advertised with grinning devils and scantily clad models, interspersed with "Sinful Unholy Love!" "Daring, Thrilling, Spicy!" and "Does a Woman Have the Right to Kill for the Man She Loves?" Another burlesque nightclub, the Driftwood, was located in East Sacramento on Thirty-third and Elvas. The Driftwood featured burlesque and strip shows, female impersonators and live surf music performed by local bands. The Driftwood was destroyed by a mysterious fire around 1970.

Traditional burlesque combined dancing with comedy skits, including male comedians and female dancers. By the 1960s, only a few remnants of the heyday of burlesque remained, with male stand-up comedians relocating to comedy clubs and dancers shifting from burlesque to striptease. Both had

Advertisement for the Pink Pussy Kat, the Orangevale strip club raided by Sheriff Misterly in 1969. *Courtesy Sacramento Public Library.*

lost customers to adult film theaters by the 1970s. A few Midtown clubs, grandfathered in prior to the policy change and outside the redevelopment zone, remained in operation, including Dave's Body Shop at Seventeenth and Broadway and the Play Room go-go club at Twenty-first and S Streets.

As a result of pressure from the City of Sacramento, strip clubs relocated to the commercial corridors of unincorporated Sacramento County or across the river in West Sacramento. Some of these clubs included the Road House in West Sacramento, Chuck Landis's Largo on Auburn Boulevard, the Fig Leaf on Power Inn Road, the Pink Pussy Kat on Greenback, the Gilded Cage and the Cottontail (inspired by the *Playboy* rabbit logo) on Fulton Avenue.

> *It* [the Cottontail] *started out as a go-go club with girls who would dance on a stage behind the bar, at the same height as the bar. I think it was the kind of place where the girl put a quarter in the jukebox, and when her song came up, she would run up to the stage and do her thing. They didn't have a live band or pre-recorded stuff, it was strictly the jukebox...I remember overhearing a conversation with my father and somebody else*

*when he explained that he owned a topless and bottomless bar and asking
him what that meant later. He explained it was a bar where the men and
women don't wear hats or shoes!*

—Mark Miller

Sheriff Misterly conducted raids of Sacramento County strip clubs, but
the Pink Pussy Kat trial drew national attention. Presiding judge was Earl
Warren Jr., son of California governor Earl Warren. He had dismissed
earlier charges in another incident in June 1969, brought against two
dancers at the Fig Leaf, but the case against Haines and Brendenson was
not as easily dismissed. The trial required two unusual changes in venue and
unique testimony. The court was convened at Chuck Landis's Largo strip
club, where expert witness Carol Doda explained the significance of nude
dancing as a form of artistic expression and demonstrated her expertise
with a live performance. A second session was convened at the Pink Pussy
Kat a Go-Go, where Haines had performed the dance that resulted in her
arrest, wearing nothing but a silver wig and a pair of pink sandals. The
jury initially found Glancy innocent but Haines and Brendenson guilty of
indecent exposure. Warren refused to accept the jury's decision and asked
them to reconsider. The second jury decision acquitted all three.

Misterly and Sacramento County district attorney John Price were
outraged, claiming Warren forced a not-guilty verdict. They did not pursue
further charges against those accused in this incident but reiterated they
would take action against any nude dancer. Glancy sought an injunction to
prevent future harassment, but U.S. District Court judge Thomas MacBride
refused to grant one. In November 1969, the county board of supervisors
banned bottomless dancing in Sacramento County, a boon to remaining strip
clubs within the Sacramento city limits that were outside Misterly's direct
reach. Dancer Suzanne Haines, one of the accused, parlayed her notoriety
into greater success on the striptease circuit. Some of the suburban clubs
switched to topless only, while others switched their format to live music
or disco dancing in order to facilitate the growing number of rock bands
seeking venues that were becoming harder to find downtown.[40]

Becoming a Public Nuisance

David Houston's earliest memory of music was his father's turning on the radio
very softly to help David sleep at night. Growing up in South Sacramento,

Public Nuisance, circa 1966–68: Ron McMaster, David Houston, Jim Matthews and Pat Mintier. *Courtesy of David Houston.*

David decided he wanted to play guitar before his hands were large enough to reach around a guitar neck, so his teacher flipped the guitar over and taught him to play slide guitar. By the time he entered Luther Burbank High School, he was playing surf guitar. The national surf craze struck particularly hard in Sacramento, where the Beach Boys were a local favorite after multiple performances at high school dances and the Memorial Auditorium. David invited his friend Jim Mathews to join him on guitar, Larry Holmes to play bass and Ron McMaster on drums. They dubbed themselves the Jaguars in 1964, built a set of surf music hits and started hunting for gigs. Options were limited for teenagers too young to play at surf bars like the Driftwood or the Candle Rock Lounge, but other opportunities emerged:

> *Southgate Shopping Center would have a battle of the bands to draw crowds of people. You had to enter the contest and I think the winner got something. We never won! We would do those and play at schools and teen centers. I don't think teen centers are too prevalent now, but they had...an*

outdoor swimming pool and a refreshment place, that was the teen center for the neighborhood. They would have dances for the kids. We played those a lot and high school dances.

When the Beatles brought the first wave of the "British Invasion," the surf-band name the Jaguars suddenly seemed old-fashioned. David and his bandmates rechristened themselves Moss and the Rocks, and Pat Mintier replaced Larry Holmes on bass. They learned a new set of British-inspired pop hits, and David became lead singer in addition to his duties as lead guitar player. They recorded a single at Ikon Studios in Sacramento titled "There She Goes" with the B-side "Please Come Back." As the band adapted to its new configuration, its sound became bluesier, grittier and louder, more like the Rolling Stones than the Beatles. In its quest for bigger and better gigs, the quartet approached Gary Schiro, the music promoter who had first brought the Beach Boys and the Rolling Stones to Sacramento. He also managed local bands, including the New Breed:

We auditioned for [Schiro]. *I think he was the one who suggested that we try a new name. There was a list, but Public Nuisance was the one that stood out. We were like one of the first punk bands. We weren't quite punk, but we were just kids who didn't know what we were doing, which is the essence of punk music. Get a guitar, turn it up loud, play, yell and scream and have fun. That's what we were doing. He had some other bands, and we presented a slightly darker image than the other ones did.*

Schiro kept Public Nuisance busy with high school dances, teen centers and local music venues like the Trip Room on the top floor of the Native Sons Hall at Eleventh and J Streets, where touring bands like Quicksilver Messenger Service and Big Brother & the Holding Company played. The band also performed at Home Front, located inside St. Paul's Episcopalian Church at Fifteenth and J Streets, across the street from Memorial Auditorium. Episcopalian priest Lee Page established Home Front as a refuge for young people in the church, which was reduced to mission status at the time and used as a social services center renamed "St. Paul's Center for Urban Studies and Ministry." Home Front shows included psychedelic light shows by Edison Lights (Don Nelson and Jim Carrico, who also designed poster art for Home Front shows) featuring local bands like heavy metal pioneers the Blue Cheer, which formed in Sacramento before moving to San Francisco. Public Nuisance also played Governor's Hall, the biggest indoor stage in Sacramento other than Memorial Auditorium, for all-ages dances.

The Native Sons Hall on Eleventh and J Streets became the Trip Room, featuring touring and local psychedelic rock bands in the late 1960s. *Center for Sacramento History,* Sacramento Bee *collection.*

Public Nuisance toured around California, securing a major label contract via producer Terry Melcher, a plan that was scuttled in 1969. Melcher, along with Beach Boys member Dennis Wilson were the previous tenants of the Tate home invaded by the Manson family, and rumors flew that Melcher was Manson's intended target. This sent Melcher into hiding, shelving all of his projects, including the Public Nuisance record. After the record debacle, the band broke up. David attempted a few other musical experiments but could not find the right combination of musicians that he had with his high school bandmates. He performed as a solo acoustic guitarist and made money teaching guitar lessons.

In 1974, David decided to buy a four-track recorder to record his own demos locally instead of driving to Los Angeles and spending $1,000 for a weekend session. He visited the Vox Room, a local music store, but the clerk encouraged him to wait five months, when TEAC was scheduled to release the first commercial 8-track recorder, the Series 70. David took his advice, purchasing a TEAC Series 70 recorder and Model 10 mixer. David was disappointed when his first recording experiments sounded nothing like a quality studio recording. He learned that, in addition to a recorder and mixer, a professional studio needed studio speakers, a professional power amplifier and high-quality microphones. Using a home amplifier and stereo speakers and microphones better suited for a gig bag than a recording studio produced inferior results. David, with the help of his parents, built an entire studio in a converted garage behind his parents' home. He christened the completed setup Moon Studios and began recording local bands. With the professional equipment, his trained ear for music, the convenience for Sacramento bands and his bargain-priced sessions at twenty-five dollars an hour, Houston became a full-time recording engineer. He moved the studio into an office near Campbell's Soup off Forty-seventh Avenue, recording an enormous number of rock and R&B albums in the 1970s and 1980s. In 1994, he lowered his overhead by moving the studio back home, recording albums for independent Sacramento bands that wanted an affordable studio that was close to home with a sound as professional as anything they could find in Southern California.[41]

JODETTE, THE "KAMELIA" OF SACRAMENTO

For many visitors to Midtown Sacramento in the 1960s, the Failasouf Shop was the embodiment of counterculture. Considered Sacramento's first "head shop," the little store at 2322 K Street carried beads, tie-dye T-shirts, incense, psychedelic posters and other fashion essentials of the Love Generation. Failasouf, the Arabic word for philosophy, was founded by legendary belly-dancer Jodette.

Born Jodette Silhi in the city of Jaffa, Jordan, to an Egyptian father and Palestinian mother, Jodette was given a French name by one of her father's customers, the French ambassador to Jordan. Her father took her to Cairo, Egypt, where she learned traditional Egyptian dance styles. She also worked in the Egyptian film industry, using the stage name "Camillia." She danced professionally at weddings and cabarets in Cairo. In the late 1950s, she returned to Jordan, dancing in Amman as well as Beirut, Lebanon. While in Amman, she was asked to perform for King Hussein. At the time, social mores prohibited dancing before the king, but King Hussein was so entranced with her singing that he asked her to dance for him. He dubbed Jodette "Kamelia of Jordan," and his favor gave her instant fame in the region and a successful career dancing in Jordan and Lebanon.

> *Beirut was the Paris of the world at my time.* 60 Minutes *said if God created heaven on Earth, he only created it in Lebanon! Which is true, it's beautiful, and I became more famous there.*
>
> —Jodette

In 1958, Jodette married an American carpenter, Carl Johnson, and moved to the United States. They chose to settle in Sacramento because Jodette's brother was attending UC Davis, one of only seven Middle Eastern students in the college at the time. For the first few years, Jodette concentrated on raising a family, and Carl got a job at the Campbell's Soup cannery. Friends in San Francisco asked Jodette to perform at a new nightclub with an Arabic theme, the Casbah, on Broadway in North Beach. Belly dancers were part of American culture dating back to the performance of "Little Egypt" at the Chicago Columbian Exposition in 1893, but according to Jodette, no performers since "Little Egypt" herself used traditional Egyptian styles, instead adapting other styles of dance that unsuccessfully imitated the traditional forms. Carl was uncomfortable with Jodette dancing for a living, but financial trouble finally convinced him to allow her to sing at the club.

> *So he make $75 a week at Campbell's Soup, $100 with overtime; I was making $75 for fifteen minutes to sing! He said, "Not only sing, dance too!" So not only was I making $75 to sing, I was making $300, $400, $500 tips! They* [threw] *at me the money because* [there was] *no singer in United States at that time* [like me]*, no Arabic dancer in United States at that time.*
>
> —Jodette

In 1962, Jodette decided that if American dancers did not know how to perform traditional Arabic styles, it was time to teach them. She had difficulties teaching at first because she spoke little English and had training as a dancer, not as a teacher. She initially taught classes at home but then moved to a studio on El Camino Boulevard in Arden-Arcade before relocating to Twenty-third and K Streets, the shop that became Failasouf. She also taught belly-dancing classes at UC Davis and on Sutter Street in San Francisco. Her classes were popular immediately due to their exotic and unusual style and the skill and experience she brought to the classroom. Jodette also performed at the California State Fair during the last years it was held at its Oak Park location, circa 1964–65, and at the Seattle World's Fair in 1974.

As the '60s progressed, Jodette grew very fond of the generation of young people who came to California in search of a different lifestyle. The Failasouf Shop and belly-dancing classes grew successful, and her clothing designs became popular throughout northern California, including with some of the biggest musical stars of the era. Jodette provided the designs while an Indian seamstress provided the labor, producing custom clothing for Janis Joplin, Jimi Hendrix, members of Jefferson Airplane and the Mamas and Papas.

Her life was also changed shortly after she signed a contract to move to Hollywood and dance at the Egyptian Garden, located on Sunset Boulevard. An auto accident on the way back to Sacramento left her unable to walk, and Jodette found herself promising God that she would give bread to the hungry every day if she could dance again. Slowly she recovered, first walking and then dancing, but she understood it was her responsibility to deliver her part of the bargain.

Many hippies arrived in Sacramento with little money or resources, on their way to San Francisco. Jodette provided food and a room in the back of Failasouf for those who lacked a place to stay, but only for a single night before they continued on their way. In 1969, she rented a retail storefront at 1802 L Street and opened a Free Shop, giving away used clothes, canned goods and domestic items. When donations fell short, Jodette sometimes gave away her own belongings. The Free Shop continued for a few years; however, a rent increase closed its doors, and Juliana's Kitchen, an organic health food restaurant, opened in its place. Jodette closed Failasouf a few years later, as the trinkets of 1960s counterculture passed from fashion, but still taught belly-dancing and continued feeding the hungry out of her dance studio.

Jodette (seated in the middle on the hood of the truck) and her dancers participate in a Fourth of July parade, circa 1974, near the corner of Tenth and K Streets. *Photo courtesy of Jodette Johnson.*

Steelwind, featuring Craig Chaquico, Danny Virdier, Francesca Gorre and Jack Traylor, performing at the Alhambra Theatre during the unsuccessful campaign to prevent the Alhambra's demolition. *Photo courtesy of Dennis Newhall.*

She and Carl opened a restaurant, Café Morocco, on Alhambra Boulevard in 1985 and opened a costume shop in 1987, a larger brick building at Twenty-second and K Streets. In 1989, Carl Johnson died, leaving Jodette in such grief that she sold the restaurant and stopped teaching dance for four years, although her students continued teaching and performing in her absence. She was finally convinced to resume teaching dance by her son, turning the shop at Twenty-second and K into her new studio. Her promise to feed the hungry never wavered.[42]

3
Far Beyond the Crocker

Encircled by its rusty iron grill
Its ragged unkempt lawn and ancient trees
Which drop dead leaves within its boundaries,
Here stands a bare and battered domicile.
The littered walks, the dry and weed-grown front,
The shuttered windows, bleak and darkened halls,
The scaling paint in tatters on its walls,
Proclaim aloud its state of least account.

Yet as a man of gentle breeding, birth,
Is still a gentleman despite his rags,
So stands this ancient manse of primate worth.
Its classic grace shines forth through mind-blown tags;
The master's thought it always must reflect
In spite of civic sloth and man's neglect.
—"The Crocker Mansion" by Harry Noyes Pratt, 1918

THE CROCKER

Built for Central Pacific Railroad lead attorney Edwin Bryant Crocker in 1873, just two years before his death, the Crocker art gallery remained in Sacramento while the art collections of other Central Pacific founders, including Leland Stanford, Collis P. Huntington, Mark Hopkins and Edwin's brother Charles, moved to San Francisco. The museum was located behind Crocker's home on Third Street, purchased from B.F. Hastings in 1868. Crocker hired local architect Seth Babson (possibly the same architect who designed the original building) to update and expand the home. Following completion of the Central Pacific Railroad, the Crocker family took a two-year vacation to Europe, returning with so much European artwork that Crocker decided to build a gallery for its exhibition, designed by Babson. The space was not solely intended as an art gallery, providing a social hall and public space befitting the wealthy Crocker family.

In 1885, Crocker's widow, Margaret, played host to the fledgling California Museum Association's first exhibition, a public show including works of art, literature and science by Jules Verne, Louis Pasteur, Auguste Renoir, Charles Dickens, Vincent van Gogh, Giuseppe Verdi and Charles Darwin. At the urging of the CMA president, Sacramento department store owner David Lubin, Margaret transferred ownership of the Crocker museum and its collection to the City of Sacramento, to ensure that the collection would not be lost after her death. Following the transfer and joint administration between CMA and the City of Sacramento, the Crocker hosted public art shows and, from 1886–96, the Crocker School of Design. While Margaret retained her residence in Sacramento for several years, she also had residences in Los Angeles, San Francisco and New York City, and in 1900–01, she gave the Crocker home to the Peniel Rescue Mission, dedicated to the care of unmarried women and their children, shortly before her death on December 1, 1901, at the age of seventy-nine. As a result of the Crocker museum and collection's transfer to the City of Sacramento, it avoided the 1906 San Francisco earthquake and fire that destroyed the collections of the other Central Pacific Railroad principals. This disaster also secured the Crocker's status as the oldest surviving art gallery in the western United States.

During the first decade of the twentieth century, local newspapers lamented the location of the Crocker, in a neighborhood that was rapidly becoming a poor immigrant neighborhood. The gallery's neighbors across Second Street were a rice mill and a cannery, part of the large industrial district along Front Street. Local news articles suggesting the relocation of the Crocker may have spurred the actions of Jennie Crocker Fassett, daughter of Margaret Crocker, who purchased the Crocker house for $20,00, and sold it to the City of Sacramento for $10,000 in 1913, relocating the Peniel Home to Colonial Heights. Between 1913 and 1918, the home remained vacant while the city considered its options, including the relocation of the

The Crocker Art Museum, circa 1970, showing the Crocker Home on the left with its 1921 Beaux Arts remodel. *Photo courtesy Vintage Sacramento, collection of W.A. Peterson.*

collection, a short-lived 1915 decision to raze the home or remodeling the existing building. During this five-year period, the house was repeatedly vandalized, and many of its furnishings stolen. In 1918, Harry Noyes Pratt, *San Francisco Chronicle* art editor and curator of the Haggin Museum in Stockton, lamented the state of the old Crocker home adjacent to the better-maintained gallery building:

> [It is a] *monument of ingratitude, how does it look to out-of-town visitors, by manner of its construction a part of the gallery. Were the house not worthy of due care, it might be a different matter, but here is one of the best bits of architecture in Sacramento, well-constructed and well worthy of preservation for itself alone, not considering its value as a reminder of Sacramento's days of romance. The writer's suggestion would be its renovation as a museum of pioneer relics and mementoes.*

In 1921, a city-funded renovation under the guidance of architect Frank Schardin stripped the Crocker home's 1860s Greek Revival ornamentation and updated it with a simpler Beaux Arts exterior and stucco finish. The corridor connecting the home to the gallery, closed during the building's period as the Peniel Home, was reopened. In 1928, Jennie donated an additional $25,000 to the museum and, between 1926 and 1929, added many items to the museum's collection. The museum board expressed its thanks to Jennie with a forty-fourth-anniversary gala in 1929.[43]

THE GREAT DEPRESSION AND SACRAMENTO ART

No, I went to Sacramento. And it's very odd. I got there and it was morning. There had been an old hotel there that had been the marvel of the days of the rich steamboats, when they ran up the river, called the Western Hotel. It was on, pretty near the waterfront. Of course, the city had grown, and that had become the slummiest place, and I said, "Well, here's a chance for me to sleep in that hotel." When I got there and registered, I could see it was just a place to hang out for the down-and-outers. But the room that I got into had great, big, high ceilings, it must have been fourteen feet high. A great tremendous bed, everything heavy furniture, and with all that I didn't sleep so well. And then I took a taxi as soon as I could and got home, and even my people didn't know me. I came here with one of these Parisian overcoats, you know, with the flaring skirts on it, and a French hat on my head and a cane and spats. It took me some time to get back into overalls again, you know, but I came over here with ten hats.
—Otis Oldfield[44]

The economic changes of the Great Depression meant new challenges for the Crocker, especially due to the relative absence of the Crocker family and other wealthy donors. William F. Jackson, museum curator and custodian of the museum since its transfer to public ownership, died in 1936. Jackson's replacement was Harry Noyes Pratt, formerly of the Haggin Museum, whose 1918 poem helped spur the Crocker home and museum's 1921 renovation. In addition to poetry, Pratt was also an author of pulp horror fiction, including "The Curse of Ximu-tal" published in the August 1930 edition of *Weird Tales* magazine. Pratt discovered that Jackson stored thousands of works in barrels in the museum basement, leading to renewed calls by the *Sacramento Union* to relocate the museum into a modern, fireproof building and out of the waterfront area. Provisional plans were made to relocate the Crocker to a new site in William Land Park, then under construction south of Sacramento, but a 1937 bond measure to fund the new museum was voted down, opposed by the Downtown and Southside Improvement Clubs. Considering the ravages of the Depression, both groups had an interest in maintaining the Crocker at the city's heart instead of a suburban relocation.[45] Following news that the Crocker was staying put, Pratt focused on the long-deferred roof repairs, electrical rewiring and an electric fire alarm in 1938 and 1939. In 1941, the Crocker home's elaborate basement was stripped of its plaster walls and ceilings due to advanced dry rot. Pratt remained curator of the Crocker until his death on May 19, 1944.[46]

William Land Park did not become home to the relocated Crocker collection, but the new park did obtain a piece of artwork by a significant California artist, sculptor Ralph Stackpole. As an instructor at the California School of the Fine Arts, one of Stackpole's closest friends was Sacramento-born artist Otis Oldfield. Oldfield, whose father was a master painter at the Southern Pacific Shops, moved briefly to San Francisco in 1908–09 before relocating to Paris to study art at the Julian Academy. Oldfield returned briefly to Sacramento in 1924, setting up a studio next to his father's home at 2127 J Street, but considered his art too far from the mainstream for success in Sacramento. He quickly moved to San Francisco, where he was reintroduced to Stackpole, whom he had met in Europe. Stackpole's sculpture was more accessible than Oldfield's challenging works like *Radical Ejaculation*, and in 1925, Stackpole won a contract to create a statue of pioneer Sacramento rancher Charles Swanston as part of a fountain in Land Park. In the following year, Stackpole won another contract to create the William Coleman Memorial Fountain in Plaza Park (now César Chávez Plaza). Stackpole was inspired by the work of Mexican muralists like José Orozco, Diego Rivera and his wife, Frida Kahlo, traveling to Mexico to see their work in 1926. They became friends, to the point that Rivera and Kahlo briefly lived with Stackpole in San Francisco, and their artistic influence is clearly visible in Stackpole's statuary and mural work in Sacramento.

As Sacramento's only postsecondary institution, Sacramento Junior College (later Sacramento City College) played an important role in the artistic life of the city. John Britton Matthew, born in Berkeley and a 1921 graduate of the Art Institute of Chicago, was hired as an art instructor at Sacramento Junior College and ran the department from 1926 until 1960. Matthew also served on the board of the Crocker and became its director in 1950. Matthew brought the Chicago Art Institute tradition of an annual artists' ball to Sacramento, organizing the junior college's first Art Ball as a fundraiser to keep art students in school. The Art Balls continued through the 1930s, and in 1937, they received operating funds from the Federal Art Project (FAP), a New Deal program intended to provide work for artists during the Depression. In conjunction with Public Works Administration funding for a new auditorium, FAP funds paid Ralph Stackpole to paint a dramatic mural in the auditorium lobby in 1937. After completing the auditorium mural, Stackpole was hired to create a frieze for the *Sacramento Bee* building on Seventh Street.[47]

The Federal Art Project also funded community art centers, and Sacramento had the first in the state. John Britton Matthew introduced FAP officials to the chamber of commerce, business leaders, the Crocker board and the superintendent of schools. FAP officials promised $10,000 annually for staff salaries if local sponsors could raise $3,000 for ongoing expenses. This goal was quickly met, and the new Art Center opened at 1422 Ninth Street on June 30, 1938. FAP sponsored artist Kathryn Uhl Ball, who first came to Sacramento to capture images of Sacramento's old waterfront in lithographs, to paint murals of dancing figures for the interior of the center. Within nine months, 1,250 students enrolled for classes, and 14,000 Sacramentans visited the center. Art classes offered included still life, landscape painting, life study, woodcarving, lettering, graphics, weaving and household product design. Later classes included mosaics, murals, theater, store window decoration, dance, flower arrangement, bookbinding, leatherwork and stonecutting.

The Art Center was also a public exhibit space beyond the crowded Crocker, featuring Federal Art Project–sponsored artists alongside the works of Rembrandt, Daumier, Van Dyck, Hogarth, Durer and Picasso. To facilitate live performances, a four-hundred-seat theater was constructed at the center in 1939. Despite the early wave of enthusiasm, the ongoing expenses of operating the center meant continued fundraising, and sponsors who were eager to contribute in 1938 were less willing to do so the following year. By the end of 1939, the center moved to smaller, less expensive quarters at 1423 H Street, and in 1941, moved temporarily to the California State Fair Dairy Building before closing entirely. Despite its short life, the center provided instruction and inspiration for several thousand young Sacramentans, including one "potential artist" identified in a 1938 photograph of the center's students: Joan Didion.[48]

STAN LUNETTA AND THE NEW MUSIC ENSEMBLE

Born in Sacramento in 1937, Stan Lunetta grew up in Oak Park on Thirty-third Street. His father played trumpet in the American Legion and Camellia

City bands, and Stan learned to play drums at an early age, playing in both marching bands while still in school. He grew up buying records from Tower Drugs, where a young Russ Solomon worked for his father before starting his Tower Records retail empire. Inspired by his high school music teacher, Aubrey Penman, Stan pursued a career in music education, but one year of junior high school music sent Stan back to college for a master's degree in music. He worked his way through college playing in Sacramento jazz bands, from a three-piece house band at the Mel-O-Dee Club to the Bill Rase Orchestra, a popular big-band jazz ensemble. Along with some of his UC Davis classmates, he formed the Concert Jazz Quintet, which played more esoteric forms of free jazz at clubs including the JayRob Theatre's suburban venue near Arden Way.

After Stan became a professor at UC Davis, his musical career took even more unusual turns. Formed in 1963, the New Music Ensemble, which performed at beatnik hangouts like the Belmonte Gallery and in conjunction with the Sacramento Symphony, consisted entirely of UC Davis Music Department faculty, but like Stan, most also played as musicians in Sacramento's jazz clubs. Their club experience and extensive collaborative jams allowed them to improvise so smoothly that it sounded like a prearranged performance.

In 1966–67, the university was actively trying to shake off its "aggie" reputation by recruiting avant-garde artists and musicians. They attracted acclaimed composer Karlheinz Stockhausen as composer in residence, followed by equally legendary composer John Cage in 1968–69. When Stan and the NME performed for Stockhausen, he originally refused to believe their performances were improvised. Stockhausen selected who would play what instrument but then changed the assignments at the last minute, like a card player switching decks on their opponent to look for signs of cheating. The New Music Ensemble players were such skilled musical cardsharps that each changed lineup still sounded smooth and professional, and Stockhausen refused to believe that they were not somehow fooling him. John Cage's composition was even more avant-garde, including pieces like *4'33"*, consisting of four minutes and thirty-three seconds of silence, with two pauses at specific points, usually indicated by closing and opening the keyboard cover of a piano on which no notes were played during the piece's duration. By this time, the sheer level of energy and experimentation around the UC Davis campus had grown to the level that Lunetta, fellow NME member Larry Austin and their group of musicians decided it was time to share their musical experiments with the world.

SOURCE: MUSIC OF THE AVANT-GARDE

The reason we ended up publishing it was that we knew a lot of people who were gifted composers, and we went, "Let's publish all these people's music along with ours!" And we started to make up a catalogue, and the catalogue got more and more…why don't we just publish a magazine? And so we did, and it was called SOURCE: MUSIC OF THE AVANT-GARDE. *The first issue, we printed 1,000, and it sold out. Second issue, we printed 2,000 and another 1,000 of the first issue.*
—Stan Lunetta

Despite publishing only eleven issues between 1967 and 1973, *SOURCE* was one of the most influential music magazines of its era, published out of Stan's basement in Poverty Ridge. Each issue of *SOURCE* was unique, experimenting not just with music but also with graphic design, page layout and printing techniques. Contributors included local Sacramento musicians alongside artists from around the world. Pages contained special folds and cutouts to accommodate special arrangements and designs. Several issues included ten-inch extended-play records bound into the magazine. *SOURCE's* refusal to follow musical convention occasionally infuriated librarians. The Boston Library staff wrote to the editors regarding issue six, whose first page was numbered 1,173, containing a score created by firing a submachine gun into sheets of musical notation paper, stating, "The first 1,172 pages are missing, and page 1,173 has got holes in it!"

The first electronic music synthesizers were introduced during this era, and *SOURCE* included many articles on electronic music with circuit diagrams and circuit board patterns so readers could create their own. Other pieces in the magazine were more conceptual, like Nelson Howe's "Fur Music," intended to be "played" by running the reader's fingers over strips of fake fur glued to the page, or a John Cage score printed on transparencies intended to be overlaid on other pages. Another score was included on a 35mm projector slide attached to a page, to be projected on a wall by the reader. Yet another consisted of a Möbius strip to be cut out and pasted together for a score of infinite length. Most scores eschewed traditional musical notation, creating their own notation methods and symbols for musical pieces unplayable by a conventional orchestra.

Other pieces were experimental to the point of danger. An environmental-music score required five ice cream trucks driving away from a central point, with prepositioned participants on nearby hilltops ready to set off flash-bang

Cover of *Source* magazine, issue six, showing the instrument used to create a musical score—a German submachinegun. *Courtesy of Stan Lunetta.*

grenades when they heard the tinkling tunes of the approaching trucks. Another simply noted, "An antipersonnel bomb, cluster type, is detonated in the audience." Slightly less hazardous was a performance based on pouring hydrogen peroxide into the listener's ear and asking them to visualize napalm sizzling flesh while the peroxide bubbled. The purpose of these bizarre, sometimes unplayable scores was to challenge the reader's concept of what a musical performance could be.

SOURCE was not strictly limited to music. Other experimental artists published work in *SOURCE*, including environmental artist Christo's early work "Valley Curtain," pioneering video artist Nam June Paik and performance art groups like Fluxus. The magazine also promoted experimental music concerts and festivals, like FFLEM (First Festival of Live Electronic Music), performed at UC Davis and Mills College in 1967, and the ICES (International Conference of Electronic Sound) festival in London, an international event featuring artists like Dick Huygens, Nam June Paik, Charlotte Moorman and Stan's performance art group AMRA/ARMA. *SOURCE* ended publication when the producers realized that each

81

issue cost so much to produce, thanks to their complex and elaborate layout, that the magazine was never profitable. Articles and scores for a twelfth issue of *SOURCE* were gathered but never published.[49]

MOOSACK MACHINES AND AMRA/ARMA

On November 21, 1969, Stan and the faculty of the UC Davis Music Department, including composer in residence John Cage, held an all-day festival of experimental music on the UC Davis campus called "Mewantemooseicday." This event featured lectures, films and performances beginning at 6:00 a.m. and ending at 12:40 a.m. This eighteen-hour, forty-minute length allowed an entire performance of early avant-garde composer Erik Satie's *Vexations*, a short theme written in 1893, played 840 times. The first live performance of *Vexations* in 1963 at the Pocket Theatre in Manhattan, coordinated by Cage, took over eighteen hours to complete. Stan Lunetta led a performance of Satie's "Furniture Music," and Cage led four sessions of a lecture entitled "How to Improve the World (You Will Only Make Matters Worse)."

The electronic devices Stan designed were called Moosack Machines. Because commercially built electronic synthesizers were still in their infancy, enormous and expensive, Stan built his own using oscillator circuits that responded to the environment around them and one another. Some of his Moosack Machines were used as part of a Crocker Art Museum exhibit in 1980. They looked like sculpture, but their artistic circuitry performed music created without direct human participation.

> *The hoops of the sculpture were really the oscillators that were making the pitches, and I stretched them out so that they were exposed to the light and the heat, and that made subtle variations on the piece. Also they looked sort of neat, with resistors and the wires sticking out. I made a mobile-type affair with them. The base had photoresistors and heat-sensitive elements and proximity detectors like they use in burglar alarms. And there was a set of spinning discs that were on little electric motors. The electric motors were turned on and off by the music, and the discs, when they spun, were spinning over the photoresistors. They had holes cut in them, so that depending on what sound came out, the motors would go on or off, and when they went on and off and the disc spun, the holes would uncover and*

Stan Lunetta (standing with pipe) and students enjoying "Mewantemooseicday" on the UC Davis campus, 1969. *Courtesy of Stan Lunetta.*

cover the photoresistors which would make different pitches in the oscillators, which would make the music different, which would make the discs turn differently—it was a big loop.

There were several places where, if you walked in front of the thing, you interrupted a light beam, and that had an effect on that whole loop. And there were heat detectors up by the air-conditioning [and] heating system

AMRA/ARMA, Stan's performance art group, posing with analog synthesizers and other noise devices, circa 1970. *Courtesy of Stan Lunetta.*

[that were] *automatic and kept going on and off to keep the room at a certain temperature. So the piece would change depending on whether the heat was on or off. There were sensors on the sides of the building so that in the morning, when the sun shone on one side, the piece sounded a certain way; then when the sun was at twelve o'clock, it sounded different; and when the sun started to go down, it sounded different again. At night, it sounded totally different, and on cloudy days, it sounded different—it was a weather indicator, too. And it played all day, every day, for six weeks.*

—Stan Lunetta[50]

AMRA/ARMA was a performance art group intended to push the musical envelope even further than NME. Stan and his musical compatriots wore otherworldly robes and helmets and staged their performances as elaborate rituals, taking on the persona of ancient "Hyborean" warriors and wizards who harnessed the chaos energies necessary to do battle with ancient Elder Gods and other unearthly monsters. AMRA/ARMA used acoustic percussion instruments and some traditional instruments combined with enormous arrays of electronic synthesizers and custom-built devices to match their inhuman costumes. These included devices like the "Runestaff," a piece of driftwood lined with electronics; a "Sound Gun" that played when its trigger was pulled; and the "Blatt Hat," a copper helmet with lights and sensors that generated tones.

As a performance art group whose work was both visual and musical, AMRA/ARMA never released an album but performed at venues including American River College, Chico State University and Sacramento's "Music Circus" theater. It also traveled to England for the 1972 ICES. The trip to ICES was documented in comic book form as a semimythical fantasy journey, illustrated by Sacramento comic artist Jeff Karl. While acts like AMRA/ARMA, NME and much of the contents of *SOURCE* were probably too "far out" for the general public, their musical experiments widened the scope of music's possibilities from Stan's basement office in Poverty Ridge. Stan continued his own musical experiments while working as a principal timpanist and percussionist for Sacramento Music Circus and Sacramento Symphony Orchestra, teaching at UC Davis and CSU Chico and music contracting for many northern California opera and choral organizations.

LA RAZA GALERIA POSADA

Esteban Villa grew up in Visalia in a family of migrant farm workers. He had a passion for books and learning, and decided to escape the migrant worker life by joining the army in 1949. His GI Bill benefits allowed him to attend the California College of Arts and Crafts in Oakland. Despite Mexican muralists' strong influence on northern California artists like Ralph Stackpole, Latino artists were not part of the curriculum. The only other Latino student at CCAC, José Montoya, shared Villa's frustration.

Mostly it was European art, Italian, Leonardo da Vinci, Michelangelo, then over in France, Matisse, Picasso and all the great French artists, Monet, Manet, artists from farther up north. They never said, we're going to study the Mexican muralists [and] *then the semester was over. When they gave me an assignment, I would seek anybody that I could identify with. I read up on Velázquez, Picasso and Salvador Dalí. I read Cervantes's* Don Quixote. *Anything that sounded like Spanish, I went for it. Even though*

*they didn't teach it in a class, I looked for this inner feeling to identify with
Spanish art, and then Mexican art. Rivera, Siqueiros, Orozco, Tamayo,
Frida Kahlo—I just devoured their books on art and murals.*
—Esteban Villa

Villa and Montoya were inspired by Mexican muralists' artistic style
and incorporated contemporary political symbols into their artwork, like
the *huelga* eagle logo of the United Farm Workers, led by César Chávez.
In 1970, Villa and Montoya were invited to teach at Sacramento State
by university administrator Manuel Alonzo. In conjunction with their
students, including Juanishi Orozco and Ricardo Favela, they formed a
Sacramento art group named the Rebel Chicano Art Front, changing the
name to Royal Chicano Air Force after the acronym's similarity to "Royal
Canadian Air Force" was mentioned.

Esteban Villa and Ricardo Favela created the first RCAF mural, located at
1400 E Street. The second RCAF mural, Esteban Villa's *Emergence of the Chicano
Social Struggle in a Bi-Cultural Society*, was painted in 1969 inside the Washington
Neighborhood Center at Sixteenth and D Streets. Because of the mural's
interior location, shielded from the weather, *Emergence* survived when other
RCAF murals were lost after long exposure to the elements or demolition.
Emergence also became an important symbol of the growing Chicano movement,
embodying what Villa called "American by birth, Chicano by choice."
Chicano artists became a bohemian counterculture, adapting the traditions of
Mexican culture to a contemporary social movement. The muralist traditions
of Mexico combined art with politics, and Chicano muralism carried on that
message as an American art form.

Villa and the RCAF saw muralism as a way to expose the community to
contemporary Chicano art, but murals were only the beginning. Both artists
received a cold reception by the university art department, which told them
there were no available classrooms for their classes. Undeterred, they utilized
neighborhood buildings to teach classes, starting with the Washington
Neighborhood Center. They later expanded to the *Centro de Artistas
Chicanas* at Thirty-second Street and Folsom Boulevard (later relocating to
2904 Franklin Boulevard) and La Raza Bookstore at 1228 F Street. The
bookstore opened in 1972 with intentions to carry books that were not
available at the Sacramento State bookstore, including ones on Mexican
art, history, literature, anthropology and sociology. Within a few years, La
Raza Bookstore became the largest and most comprehensive bookstore of
its kind in the nation. Starting in a Queen Anne Victorian home, in 1980,

La Raza Bookstore at 1226 F Street also served as an art gallery, with Royal Chicano Air Force murals decorating the exterior. *Photo by Joe Perfecto.*

The Sacramento *Concilio* social service agency at Nineteenth and F Streets featured a mural by RCAF member Juanishi Orozco. *Photo courtesy Vintage Sacramento, collection of W.A. Peterson.*

the bookstore expanded into a vacant space next door. The bookstore's art gallery was named La Raza Galeria Posada, named for Mexican artist and printmaker José Guadalupe Posada.[51]

The RCAF's screen printing facilities were used to create materials promote their events, community events and even local political campaigns. Phil Isenberg's city council and mayor campaign posters were produced by the RCAF via his friendship with RCAF member Joe Serna. Isenberg, along with council member Burnett Miller, helped create the Sacramento Metropolitan Arts Commission, a city-affiliated nonprofit to administer public art grants, and a program called "Art in Public Places." This program was originally envisioned by Esteban Villa and other RCAF artists as a 3 percent assessment on new construction to be set aside for public art in new Sacramento City and County buildings. As passed in 1977, the assessment was reduced to 2 percent. Thanks to their experience with public art and muralism, RCAF members were able to obtain significant commissions for city and county projects. Environmental artist Horst Leissl was the recipient of several "Art in Public Places" grants, including installation of an enormous fly on the Alhambra Boulevard water tank in East Sacramento and Egyptian-style paintings of ibises along the concrete levee walks along the Sacramento River in Old Sacramento. When Joe Serna ran for city council and mayor, his campaign posters were also printed by the RCAF. Serna became Sacramento's first Latino mayor in 1991, and during his time as a city council member and as mayor, Serna worked to advocate for the RCAF's causes. In 1992, Serna was instrumental in helping La Raza Galeria Posada move into the Heilbron Mansion at Seventh and O Streets.[52]

The year 1992 also brought a new artist group, *Las Co-Madres Artistas*. Founded by Carmel Castillo, Helen Villa, Irma Lerma Barbosa, Laura Llano, Mareia de Socorro and Simona Hernández, the Co-Madres emerged to reinforce the voice of Chicana artists. Irma Barbosa was an early member of the RCAF but felt dissatisfied with its underrepresentation of female artists.

> *Over the years I saw that women were not given the same opportunities to exhibit or to celebrate their creativity. Their work was not recognized. It wasn't visible. I was toasted as the only female that exhibited with the Royal Chicano Air Force, the original group. At first it felt like an honor, later it felt very lonely. As time went on, I, like all of my comadres, went on my way and fulfilled my duties: raising children, getting a job and still contributing to the community, but [I] still [felt] very invisible.*
>
> —Irma Barbosa

In 1992, La Raza Galeria Posada relocated to the Heilbron Mansion at Seventh and O Streets, with the help of Mayor Joe Serna. *Center for Sacramento History,* Suttertown News *collection.*

Asked by Sandra Martínez of Sacramento City College to participate in an exhibit, Irma invited Simona Hernández, a Sacramento State graduate who grew up in Roseville; Carmel Castillo, who grew up visiting the Crocker as a small child when the nearby neighborhood was still part of the Sacramento *barrio*; and Helen Villa, wife of Esteban Villa, who promoted her husband's art for years instead of promoting her own. They were joined by Mareia de Socorro, a retired social worker who had deferred her own interest in art to raise a family and pursue a career, and Laura Llano, an

Luna's Café on Sixteenth Street often served as a gallery for *Las Co-Madres Artistas,* interpreted here as an outpost of Chicana culture by Mareia de Socorro. *Painting by Mareia de Socorro.*

artist and storyteller who sometimes dressed as master artist Frida Kahlo to demonstrate to her students Kahlo's importance in the art world. In 1975, Socorro and Laura Llano, along with Mary McGrath, opened the Omega Gallery, Sacramento's first Chicana-owned art gallery. Groups like the RCAF and Co-Madres represented part of the reason why American society produced a larger proportion of artists in the late twentieth century. Nonwhites and women tore down the social barriers that prevented them from pursuing creative careers and artistic expression, making a place for themselves in the city's artistic legacy.[53]

4

Feeders of the Arts

Cities need old buildings so badly it is probably impossible for vigorous streets and districts to grow without them…Well-subsidized opera and art museums often go into new buildings. But the unformalized feeders of the arts—studios, galleries, stores for musical instruments and art supplies, backrooms where the low earning power of a seat and table can absorb uneconomic discussions—these go into old buildings…As for really new ideas of any kind—no matter how ultimately profitable or otherwise successful some of them might prove to be—there is no leeway for such chancy trial, error and experimentation in the high-overhead economy of new construction. Old ideas can sometimes use new buildings. New ideas must use old buildings.
—*Jane Jacobs,* The Death and Life of Great American Cities[54]

The JayRob Theatre opened in a former winery at 1513 Eighteenth Street and became one of Sacramento's most successful small theater groups. Founded by Justus Wyman and his son, Robert, "JayRob" was a simple combination of its founders' names. In the early 1950s, Sacramento's theatrical establishment pursued funds to build two purpose-built theaters, the Music Circus and the Eaglet. In the interim, theater groups used inexpensive old buildings

Established in 1881 by Portuguese immigrant Manuel Nevis, the Eagle Winery was a two-story, 66- by 120-foot brick building topped by a corrugated metal roof built by carpenter Nicholas Harvie. Nevis opened several more wineries in Sacramento and transferred the Eagle to his cousins Manuel and Joaquim Azevedo in 1888–89.[55] The Azevedo family operated

Above: A JayRob Theatre production of *The Tender Trap*, featuring, left to right: Diana Lyons, Joanne Blomberg, John Ickes, Carolyn Wiley and Betty Anderson. *Photo courtesy of Diana Wyman.*

Left: Studio portrait of William J. Geery, circa 1940, during his Broadway career. *Photo courtesy of Diane Heinzer.*

the winery until about 1918. From the 1920s to the 1940s, the building housed assorted businesses, including an auto garage and a candy company, Elmo's Wholesale Confectionery. By 1949, the Sacramento Civic Repertory Theatre Workshop moved into Elmo's. The Sacramento Civic Rep formed in 1942 to entertain locally stationed troops during World War II, and in the war years, it utilized several ad hoc spaces for its performances. In October 1949, it moved into the new Eaglet Theatre at Fourteenth and H Streets, and in 1950, the old winery became the Theatre Studio, a name it carried until 1956.[56]

Justus Wyman was born in Richmond, California, in 1908, leaving home for the vaudeville circuit in 1924. Justus married Alice Frankel, a ballet dancer who sang and danced with her sisters on the vaudeville circuit. From 1929 until 1940, Justus wrote, produced, directed and managed plays in San Francisco. The family moved to Sacramento in 1941. In 1947, Justus began his three years of producing plays at McClellan Air Force Base; coordinated an early television series for KCCC, Sacramento's first television station; and produced *These Are Your Neighbors* for KBET, a television station owned by the McClatchy Company, the parent company of the *Sacramento Bee*. The Wymans' son, Robert, started in show business at age seven. After graduating from Sacramento State with his Master of Arts, Robert, along with his father, decided to open a theater. They chose the Theatre Studio in the old winery based on its existing familiarity to theater patrons and its low rental price of ten dollars per performance, reduced from twenty-five dollars by the theater's owner, Elissa Sharee.

Productions at the JayRob were usually popular shows with origins on Broadway, despite the Wymans' West Coast roots, suited to the theatrical tastes of Sacramento's new suburban middle class. The 1956 season plays included *Oh Men! Oh Women!*, *The Tender Trap*, *The Seven Year Itch*, *The Moon Is Blue* and *The Little Hut*. Reviews of the JayRob's performances were very strong, leading to sold-out shows. The little winery-theater's maximum capacity of 150 limited the company's potential for growth, so the JayRob moved to the Little Theatre, a 290-seat theater adjacent to Memorial Auditorium's main hall, in 1958. These performances were equally well received, encouraging the Wymans, in 1961, to build a theater closer to many of their patrons at Sacramento Inn Plaza near Arden Way. The old winery continued as the Theatre Studio into the 1960s.

The JayRob's marketing and advertising materials were professionally produced and designed. Its first few programs were simple handbills, but by the end of its first season, it had secured the services of Geo/Louie Associates, a graphic design company with a distinct Modernist style. Louie's work was frequently seen in advertisements for Sacramento jazz clubs—including the Clayton Club and the Mo-Mo Club—the Del Prado restaurant and real estate ads for Del Paso Manor. In its third season, the JayRob retained the services of equally talented graphic designer Audrey Tsuruda. Born Audrey Yee in New York City, she moved to Sacramento in 1944 with her father, Kim John Yee, who opened a Hawaiian barbecue restaurant, John's Rendezvous, at Seventeenth and L Streets. Returning to New York for design school, she married a handsome Japanese American soldier and returned to Sacramento to start her career. She overcame prejudice against women and Asians in the graphic design profession, co-founding Tsuruda/Read and Others Advertising in 1964 and founding her own agency, Tsuruda Group, in 1979. With her business partner Maurice Reid, Audrey's design firm was one of the first in California to specialize in political campaigns.[57]

THE PEASE CONSERVATORY AND THE SHOW BELOW

Located at 2130 L Street, the Pease Conservatory was located in a dramatic Queen Anne home built in 1899 for Edward James Carraghar, owner of the Saddle Rock restaurant on Second Street and Democratic Party political boss, who served on the city's board of trustees. In 1921, the home was purchased by Edward Pease and his wife, Zuelina Geery Pease. Edward established a music school in the Odd Fellows' Hall on Ninth and K in 1914; however, traffic and noise made instruction difficult, so they relocated to the Carraghar home. Lessons were taught on the main floor while the Pease family lived upstairs. The basement was converted into a recital room seating one hundred. Live performances were broadcast on KFBK via a small broadcast studio in the basement.

In 1949, Zuelina hired her nephew William Geery as a voice instructor. Geery had recently returned from New York, where he performed in Broadway shows, and married pianist Lenore Wiren. In addition to teaching at the music school, he acted at the Music Circus, bringing his Broadway experience to Sacramento. In 1968, Zuelina Pease could no longer maintain the facility, so Geery moved his family into the conservatory and took charge of the school. Some of his friends from the local theater world approached him about using the conservatory basement as a small theater. The space was reconfigured with forty-nine seats and opened as Sacramento

William J. Geery, circa 1950–55, dressed for a role at Music Circus. *Photo courtesy of Diane Heinzer.*

Experimental Theatre in 1972. From 1986 until 1996, the theater was called the Show Below and leased by Charles Slater, veteran of the Chautaqua theater company at R and Twenty-fifth Street and the basement theater of the YWCA on Seventeenth and L Streets. Unlike the Music Circus or the JayRob, the theater companies at the Show Below preferred original, unconventional and locally produced plays, better suited for a small stage. In 1996, the Show Below changed management and was renamed after Geery, who died in 1993. Geery's stepdaughter Diane Heinzer and her husband, Jon, took over management of the conservatory and theater, moving into the Pease family space upstairs.

FROM AEROJET TO HOLLYWOOD: PAT MORITA

Born in 1932 in Isleton, Sacramento County, Noriyuki "Pat" Morita overcame a childhood of tragedy through his gift for comedy. From age two until eleven, Pat lived in a sanitarium in Weimar, California, where he was treated for spinal tuberculosis. When discharged in 1943, he was sent directly to an internment camp in Arizona and later to another camp at Tule Lake, California. In addition to the indignity of imprisonment just as he recovered from nine years of illness, young Pat did not speak Japanese and had to attend school with six-year-olds in order to learn his family's language. Pat had already demonstrated an indomitable spirit in the sanitarium, adopting a well-developed sense of humor to overcome his physical ailment. He created and performed satirical comedy routines as a way to poke fun at the ridiculous injustice of internment.

After the war, Pat graduated from Fairfield High School at age sixteen, and attended Sacramento City College for the next two years, planning to study medicine, but in 1950, he left college to help his family open a restaurant. Because Japanese food was very unpopular in the years following World War II, the restaurant, Ariake Chop Suey, served Chinese food. Located at 1323 Fourth Street in the mixed-race neighborhood of the old West End's Japantown, his customers were black, Filipino and Mexican in addition to Japanese and Chinese. This exposed Pat to a multitude of ethnic accents and mannerisms that he learned to mimic for comedy routines, making his customers into test audiences for jokes. In 1952, the same year his father closed his restaurant, Pat married Kathleen Yamachi. He sought more lucrative employment than waiting tables, securing a job at Aerojet in Rancho Cordova. He advanced rapidly in Aerojet's computer division, earning $10,000 a year as a department head. In his spare time, he performed stand-up comedy at nightclubs in Sacramento and the Bay Area and acted as master of ceremonies at weddings. In 1962, a friend offered

Pat Morita got his start in comedy and acting in Sacramento, making the jump from Aerojet manager to stand-up comedian. *Author's collection.*

Pat an $800-per-month job acting as master of ceremonies at Ginza West, a new comedy club in San Francisco. Pat took the leap from high technology to stand-up comedy and never looked back.

By 1967, Pat was one of the hottest comedians on the national circuit, performing at the Copacabana in New York, the Tropicana in Las Vegas,

Mr. Kelly's in Chicago and the Playboy Clubs, earning $1,000 per week, five times his handsome Aerojet salary. Part of his success as a comedian may have been due to the crumbling racial barriers of the civil rights era and his dismantling of racial stereotypes through comedy. Pat was also able to charm audiences and deconstruct serious subjects with humor, including a 1966 performance in Hawaii, at which, moments before taking the stage, Pat realized he was performing in front of a group of disabled veterans present for the Twenty-fifth anniversary of Pearl Harbor. Pat's opening line, "Before I begin, I just want to say I'm sorry about messing up your harbor," was met by a brief, stunned silence, followed by a wave of laughter.

The year 1967 also brought Pat's first movie role, a small part in *Thoroughly Modern Millie*. By the 1970s, he had become one of the earliest well-known Japanese American actors. He became a regular on the series *Happy Days* and starred in two of the first television series with an Asian American lead character, the comedy *Mr. T and Tina* and the police drama *Ohara*. Morita was best known for his role as Mr. Miyagi in *The Karate Kid*, a performance that earned him an Oscar nomination. That role captured his talent for natural humor and ability to break down racial stereotypes, as well as an iconic scene in which Miyagi, a veteran of World War II's 442nd Regimental Combat Team (the only Japanese American unit to fight in World War II), mourns his wife and child who died in an internment camp. Morita died in 2005.[58]

THE ORIGINAL MIDTOWN BEATNIK: VICTOR WONG

Victor Wong was born in San Francisco's Chinatown in 1927, but much of his early childhood was spent in the Sacramento Delta towns of Courtland and Locke, where his father had a job as school principal and teacher to the children of the Sacramento Delta's Chinatowns. Victor participated in the nascent Beat movement in San Francisco's North Beach and attended UC–Berkeley, where he studied journalism and political science. He studied theology at the University of Chicago, but left graduate school in 1961 to join the Chicago "Second City" comedy troupe. Wong disliked Chicago's enormous size, explaining that "this was the first time that I had ever gone someplace where I couldn't get home within 15 minutes. I got scared. I was scared all the time." He also felt disrespected by other members of the Second City troupe due to his race. "That was the times. The early sixties—you barely had heard about *Brown vs. Board of Education*. I had only Asian parts."[59]

Returning to San Francisco, Wong acted in local theater and continued his graduate studies at the San Francisco Art Institute under Mark Rothko. Wong also spent time with the Beat poets of the era, including Jack Kerouac, who based Arthur Ma, a character in his novel *Big Sur*, on Victor. Wong also became a journalist and newscaster on public television station KQED. His journalism career was cut short due to Bell's palsy, a neurological affliction that gave his face a sagging, lopsided appearance. This disorder deeply troubled Victor, but he overcame it by shifing from journalism to acting, on stage and in movies, ranging from Shakespeare to action films and comedies. In 1980, just as his movie career began to take off and after a brief sojourn in China, Victor moved from San Francisco to Midtown Sacramento.

Victor's sons lived in Sacramento, one of his justifications for the move, and he liked the built environment. "I like Sacramento a lot. It reminds me of Paris. You know, the alleys, the trains coming through, the weather," he said to an interviewer with the *Suttertown News*. He quickly became a regular figure at Midtown Sacramento coffee shops, poetry readings and art galleries. Deeply spiritual and unconventional, Wong was unimpressed by Hollywood's displays of ostentatious wealth, preferring a simpler life. When asked about why he did not live in Hollywood, he said, "I drive a 1972 Plymouth. I've always had used cars. I have a self-imposed vow of poverty. Hollywood is an awful place. People are always back-stabbing. Being of Chinese descent, I wouldn't go into that kind of Hollywood thing. I wouldn't want to be part of that." Victor was more enthusiastic when asked about Midtown: "It was like the early days of the Beatniks in San Francisco. The energy was very high, people were staying up all night talking to each other. There were poetry readings, and there were gallery shows every week, where all the artists would go and talk and argue and eat food all night."

Victor had great success in Hollywood but remained part of the Midtown creative scene. In 1990, he joined the K-RAP Radio Players, a small troupe that included Wong, David Spangen'Burg, John Spritz, Margret Boone, Randall Snatch and Chris McDonald. They performed at Drago's Café and Melarkey's, creating a two-act "radio play" set in the studio of fictitious independent radio station K-RAP, the voice of "Sacrademento." Originally intended as a solo monologue for Wong, the production evolved into the disjointed story of a radio announcer dealing with comical interruptions from multiple sources. Live performances of K-RAP often included improvisational participation by members of the audience, adding a dynamic

Above: *Left to right*: Victor Wong, Margret Boone, David Spangen'Burg, John Spritz, Randall Snatch and Chris McDonald, the K-RAP Radio Players, at Drago's Café, 2326 K Street. *Center for Sacramento History*, Suttertown News *collection*.

Left: A cargo bike in front of Juliana's Kitchen organic restaurant, with a Mickey Abbey stained-glass piece in the window, captures essential elements of Midtown: cycling, art and cafés. *Photo courtesy of Mickey Abbey.*

and unpredictable element. Wong lived in Sacramento until the late 1990s, moving back to the Delta to live in Locke with his fourth wife, Dawn Rose. He died on September 12, 2001.[60]

MIDTOWN '81

It was the punk era, and there was a lot of nihilism then. There were performances and expression about destruction and destruction being OK. We saw it in the young people [who] *were piercing themselves, and they were hurting themselves, a lot of them, and that was supposedly cool…A lot of energy that came out of the punk movement was in the arts.*
—Marco Fuoco

In *The Warhol Economy*, Elizabeth Currid examined the importance of New York's arts community to the city's economic life. She outlined how the factors that led to the city's economic collapse in the mid-1970s were the same as those that allowed artists to cluster in the same neighborhoods, paying low rents that let them focus on performance and artwork. These low rents also allowed small, semilegal venues and galleries to operate below the official radar in low-rent industrial and retail spaces, resulting in a small but tightknit group in which artists and musicians were free to experiment, if they were willing to accept a relatively small audience and tolerate the environmental hazards of a decaying Downtown. Dangerous neighborhoods meant cheap rent, for housing and for businesses with marginal returns, and the Lower East Side became a hotbed of artistic creativity. CBGB, a tiny bar in the Bowery, became a musical mecca, and street artists progressed from graffiti to gallery openings. City officials were more concerned with bigger problems than unlicensed music venues or guerrilla artists staging events in vacant buildings. The independent film *Downtown '81* provided a snapshot of the Lower East Side's "No Wave" culture.

Even in New York, the core group of the Lower East Side was limited to a few hundred people in the neighborhood. They formed bands with one another, collaborated on films and art, formed sexual relationships and friendships and attended group members' shows. Once the members of this network achieved sufficient critical mass to connect with the larger art world, they attracted attention from New York's established art galleries, music and film companies. A limited number of these artists found commercial success, at the cost of higher rents and less room for unfettered creativity. On a smaller scale, Downtown Sacramento faced many of the same challenges as inner-city New York. Artists appeared in galleries and informal spaces, wherever art would fit.[61]

By the late 1970s, the end of the hippie era meant the decline or closure of some of Sacramento's art galleries. Those that focused on crafts and functional items, like the Beginning at Seventeenth and L Streets and in the Building on R Street, were able to survive, but fine art galleries struggled to reach an audience who seldom traveled Downtown. The Beginning's longtime neighbors, Le Sahuc Gallery at 1727 L Street, closed its doors in 1978 after a nine-year run. Focusing on Funk Art, it had difficulty attracting patrons and art-buying customers, while the Candy Store Gallery in Folsom became the most successful art gallery in the region.[62]

In the late 1970s and early 1980s, artists created temporary art spaces and events. In May 1981, the Open Ring Gallery held a "Tongue-in-Chic" fashion show above Bud's Buffet at 1020 Tenth Street, featuring thirty artists and designers combining the city's chic elite and its artistic riffraff. The event was narrated by B.T. Collins, Jerry Brown's chief of staff and a former Green Beret. The show featured a "Surf and Turf" ensemble, combining cowboy and Hawaiian styles, including grass chaps, an "Impregnation Coat" created by miniaturist Dolph Gotelli, a dinner jacket with candelabra epaulets, a Wedgwood necktie, a hat made of sourdough bread (for those who eat on the run) and a Philip Morris smoking jacket.

Also in 1981, Reverend Robert Lee and his wife, Reverend Alice, founded the Church of the Immaculate '60 Chevy, a "clench" of the Church of the SubGenius, a Dallas-based national network of bold surrealists following the teachings of J.R. "Bob" Dobbs group, promoted by Reverend Ivan Stang. The Subgenii drew artists and creative individuals via clip-art based propaganda and "Media Barrage" mix tapes. Reverend Lee attended the first SubGenius convention in Dallas and brought the church to Sacramento, where he made a living as a jeweler, selling custom-made silver Dobbshead icons. On January 22, 1983, a group of Sacramento artists held a "Night of Kafka," a celebration of the hundredth anniversary of Franz Kafka's birth. The event featured a "Franz Kafka Think-Alike Contest," music by the Reinhard String Trio and readings of Kafka's work, with wine, champagne and hors d'oeuvres.[63]

More formal Downtown galleries also appeared during the early 1980s. The Jennifer Pauls Gallery opened in the Open Ring Gallery's space at 1020 Tenth. Michael Himovitz and Hillel Salomon took

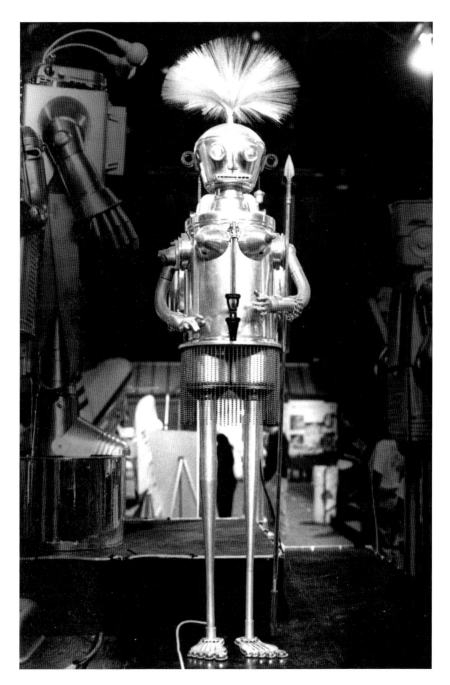

Clayton Bailey's robot sculptures were featured at art shows at Cal Expo and Crocker Art Museum alongside robots designed by Stucco Factory robot expert Gene Oldfield. *Center for Sacramento History,* Suttertown News *collection.*

over the space in 1984, putting on shows featuring Gary Pruner, Robert Brubaker and Suzanne Adan and themed shows like "Use Me," a show dedicated to functional art. In 1992, Himovitz relocated to a new studio on Del Paso Boulevard, citing a lack of parking, an influx of street people and a lack of investment in his stretch of K Street. His gallery was a regular stop on Sacramento's annual Art Walk, a tradition begun in 1984. In 1993, Himovitz pioneered the idea of making the annual event monthly, known as Second Saturday. He died in 1994 of complications due to HIV/AIDS, but his gallery, and the monthly Art Walk, survived.[64]

Other tragedies in the art community occurred more suddenly. On September 10, 1985, artist Fred Uhl Ball, son of muralist Kathryn Uhl Ball, the muralist who came to Sacramento as part of the Federal Art Project, was attacked outside his studio at 1727 I Street, dying of his injuries two months later. He was a well-respected muralist with works throughout California and in private collections throughout the country and had authored a 1972 work on techniques in enamel, considered the standard work on the subject. His Sacramento work included *The Way Home*, an enamel mural on the parking garage on Third and L Streets. Ball's death after an apparently unprovoked attack was a reminder that Midtown Sacramento was still a sometimes dangerous place, a factor many considered an acceptable tradeoff for low rent.[65]

THE STUCCO FACTORY

Brian Gorman's first gallery was located in his own apartment at 3655 J Street above J. Prassa Printers in 1979. In conjunction with a friend, Tower Books employee Dylan Garcia, he opened a space above Levinson's Books Downtown at 1016 Tenth Street, the Fido Gallery. By 1980, artists Christine Manz, Sue Tonkin and Sheila Sullivan had studios there. Sullivan described Sacramento's art scene of the era: "[L]ots of people are doing interesting things, but nobody knows about it…the pace is relatively slow so there is not a lot of pressure to produce marketable work. The same old dumb things happen every year in Sacramento competitions. The awards go to the good but safe works."[66]

Shortly after opening, poet Bari Kennedy asked if he could hold poetry readings at their new space. Gorman agreed, but the wild poetry events infuriated Garcia, who was less comfortable with company. Down the street from Gorman and Garcia, young artist Steve Vanoni had a space at the

Steve Vanoni, prolific artist and musician, was an early resident of the Stucco Factory. *Photo by George Westcott.*

IXL Building at Seventh and J Streets, a tiny studio in a gigantic building. By 1983, Gorman decided they needed a larger space that provided enough room for exhibits, studios and places to sleep in relative peace. Exploring Midtown by bicycle, Gorman found a vacant industrial building, a former stucco company, near Twenty-seventh Street along the R Street railroad corridor. So Gorman called the owners and asked to rent the space.

It was $500 a month for a fourteen-thousand-square-foot warehouse and eight thousand [square feet] *of land. So Vanoni and me and* [Gary] *Dinnen were in the place for the first year. And then after that they raised the rent to $1,000, and we had to rent out spaces. It was basically warehouse space. We had a little outhouse toilet in this big courtyard, big gigantic double doors that opened out onto R Street and a loading dock we used as a stage when we had a band.*

—Brian Gorman

The Stucco Factory, as it became known, quickly attracted more artists, helping divide the rent. Painter Gary Dinnen was an early tenant, along with electronics whiz and artist Harrison Thomas and actor/artist Victor Wong. Wong's stepson Charlie Aitken installed a recording studio in a Stucco Factory space. Dinnen, Wong, Aitken and Thomas started their own arts group, Diversion Island Video, and created a short film about cannibalism in Sacramento titled *Death by Jealousy*. The Fido Gallery was relocated as Stucco's gallery space, featuring art receptions and themed events including the Second Artists Canine Fashion Extravaganza, a gala event with work by local artists and designers. The fashion show featured humans dressed as dogs and dogs dressed as humans, a tradition carried on from a similar show held at the old Fido Gallery on Tenth Street. The Stucco Factory was also used as practice space by local bands and sometimes for parties and live music events, strictly without official permits. The "house band" was the Nebulous Stucco Thing, an ever-changing lineup of poets, musicians and performance artists. Not all their events took place in the Stucco Factory; on July 28, 1987, Gorman and Steve Vanoni organized the Marcel Duchamp Classic, a celebration of the 100th birthday of Dada artist Marcel Duchamp, in Plaza Park.[67] The Stucco Factory also encouraged new arrivals to Sacramento to launch their own art projects.

My best friend Penny moved down from Grass Valley and my parents co-signed for an apartment [at Q and Seventeenth]. *It was $325 a*

This 1983 sketch by Arthur Balderama advertised the second-annual Artists' Canine Fashion Extravaganza at Fido Art Gallery, the Stucco Factory's exhibit space. *Courtesy of Brian Gorman.*

month, two bedroom[s]. We both slept in one bedroom and used the other as our creative art space. The first thing we did was have a raging party. We [didn't] care if we get thrown out, we just want[ed] to meet people and have our own "coming out" party in Sacramento. That's where we met Duncan Wong, [and] he brought Steve Vanoni, Harrison Thomas, Pete Wedel, Charlie Aitken—we met a ton of people! We didn't get thrown out, but it was a hell of a party! We had the party on a Friday, and we spent all day Saturday making art with some of the people who came to the party…Derek Lively, who was in Tales of Terror. *So we just made all these friends, just the weirdos from Downtown…I remember being the door person for the Stucco Factory, Nebulous Stucco Thing would have shows and sometimes I'd be the door girl.*

—Heidi "Kizzy" Miller

Sacramento had little interest in cracking down on artists in a warehouse during the early 1980s when other regional priorities gathered more civic attention. But by the 1990s, real estate firms had become interested in Downtown development, including the R Street corridor. Unlicensed artistic shenanigans were less well received. On August 1, 1993, a fire broke out at the Stucco Factory, quickly engulfing the building. Victor Wong, who lived nearby, witnessed the fire, telling a *Sacramento Bee* reporter, "It's so sad—it used to be an art community in the '80s. I used to have a band and we practiced there. There was a lot of history to that place." Stucco Factory founder Brian Gorman suspected that arson played a role in the building's destruction.[68]

I used to go to the shows there. That was a little bit before I moved down here. It was always sort of like another world. If you went there at night, it was not necessarily well lit, and there were a lot of corners, a lot of junk around, mannequins, car parts. If you were coming from the suburbs and trying to get out of there, it was a pretty exotic place to be.

—Mark Miller

DUMPSTER GODS ON R STREET

Farther west on R Street, another group of artists started another multimedia space similar to the Stucco Factory in the summer of 1987, the R Street Complex. Located in the old Perfection Bakery on Fourteenth and R, a two-story brick building, the complex featured a team of artists, including robotics expert Gene Oldfield; artists Kele Duncan, Cassandra Manzo and Eric Bianchi; musician Steve Passarell; and music promoter Jerry Perry. Its inaugural event was Gallery SoToDo's "Fourth of July Political Art Show," featuring ninety-one works of art, live performance art, and a spontaneous election of Sacramento's "Art Mayor," a title won easily by Midtown scrivener Ground Chuck. In September 1987, artist Steve Vanoni displayed a ten-year retrospective of his artwork. The space also featured live bands promoted by Jerry Perry, including Vicious Gel, the Squishies, the Boorman 6, I Love Ethyl, Pride and Peril and Slack. The space also hosted elaborate theme parties, including "Jimi Hendrix Memorial Night" and a disco-themed "Sucking on the Seventies Night."

Marco Fuoco moved from Philadelphia to Sacramento in 1979, opening Random Access Gallery on Del Paso Boulevard, later relocating to the IDEA (Institute for Design and Experimental Art) Gallery at 824½ J Street, opened by relocated Los Angeles artist Claudia Chapline.[69] "We were feral artists," said Fuoco. "Blood and guts were out on the street." He created video art

Marco Fuoco and Billie Moreno at a fashion show and AIDS benefit held at the Crest Theatre, circa 1985. *Photo by George Westcott.*

installations, statues with television heads that showed distorted video of faces, and became involved with a later incarnation of the Nebulous Stucco Thing called the Screaming Pygmy Orchestra. Fuoco also pursued National Endowment for the Arts grant funding to create "Dumpster Gods" in 1989, a movie about a man in a vinyl suit who bicycles around Sacramento, encountering characters like Ray Rill and Ground Chuck. He felt his NEA grant's timing was lucky:

> *In those days, the NEA grants, before "Piss Christ"* [a controversial NEA-funded photograph by Robert Mapplethorpe], *I got the grant the same year. If they would have kicked out "Dumpster Gods," I would have been famous! After that, that was it—there was no more NEA. You couldn't grant weird stuff anymore, and in those days, that was the granddaddy of grants! It was quite an honor—they gave me $5,000.*

For Sacramento's feral artists and social aliens, the Crocker was often out of reach. Via social connections and underground art venues, the lines between art forms became blurred, and groups of artists, musicians, poets and other creative people collaborated in shared spaces. Old Victorian houses, retail storefronts and industrial buildings in Downtown Sacramento became theaters, art galleries, studios, music venues and homes. In their search for a living space with artistic flexibility and low rent, they were willing to tolerate poor living conditions and the risk of official expulsion. Some artists called for changes to city codes to legalize the use of these marginal industrial spaces as living and working spaces, but Sacramento's artists lacked the political power to execute these ideas, or the economic power via patronage to draw attention to their cause. The business community saw these buildings as examples of blight to be cleared away and saw little value in the buildings or their bohemian inhabitants. For the older Sacramento elite, art belonged inside the Crocker, until the outsider artists brought art to the streets.

As Midtown Sacramento became more marketable and popular, the art scene became more competitive, due in part to its growing number of artists. With notoriety came attention from real estate developers who saw the value of Downtown and Midtown based on its location and land, not the buildings or people who were already there. IDEA Gallery, including Marco Fuoco's studio, closed in 1986 after the building's new owner tripled the rent.[70] Rising rents and loss of art spaces changed the nature of the art scene. According to Fuoco, "The wind kind of blew through town, and it was gone in '91."

Bobby Burns and Kizzy Miller on an Easter "Beer Hunt." Participants hid artistically decorated beer cans and hunted them down, consuming each beer before continuing the hunt. *Photo courtesy of Mara Wagner.*

The outsider spirit of the 1980s ebbed, but the Sacramento art scene grew as another generation came of age, focusing its efforts on locations farther east in Midtown.

> *The community became very commercially self-conscious, and at the same time, the artists and poets began bickering with each other. Suddenly everything was getting yuppified, and the artists were too busy fighting each other to defend themselves. The galleries now—they're wall-to-wall carpet, they don't serve food at openings and the artists don't go there anymore…The money people started coming back Downtown. And they're not sharing; they're just pushing the artists and poets out. The secret to a healthy cultural life is that it's a marriage—and in Sacramento art and society haven't found each other.*
>
> —Victor Wong[71]

5

Urban Pioneers

*What makes Sacramento great is that it has soul…and that's us. We want to
bring back what we've lost.*
—Marilyn Dressler[72]

*I don't know of a single house which has to be torn down. We could double the
population in the Downtown area without tearing down a single building.*
—Bill Atherton, former president of Sacramento Old City Association[73]

YOUNG PEOPLE IN THE OLD CITY

In the 1960 City of Sacramento General Plan, the entire Old City was zoned
for high-density residential or commercial use, making the existing stock of
single-family homes noncompliant uses of the land on which they stood. Tax
laws incentivized demolition, and city building officials refused to approve
renovations of old buildings that did not meet the latest building codes,
often assuming they should be demolished outright. As a new generation of
young professionals moved to Sacramento, they saw a neighborhood worth
saving, but they were barred from traditional financing. Their education and
willingness to organize opened new doors and changed the way the city
thought about Downtown Sacramento. In 1972, a group of about half a
dozen families formed the Sacramento Old City Association as a means to
share tools, information and mutual support.

Left to right: Delphine Cathcart, Tony Magennis, Paul and Marcella Cathcart and Jim Cathcart on the porch of 2409 H Street. Magennis helped teach SOCA members how to use "Stuckee" financing to purchase redlined homes. *Center for Sacramento History,* Suttertown News *collection.*

In January 1969, Jim Cathcart moved to Sacramento for a job as chief consultant to the California Senate's Business and Professions Committee. He sought an apartment nearby so he could walk to work but found that very few were available to families. According to Jim, "In those days, there were no dogs allowed, no children allowed." With some persistence, he found an apartment for himself; his wife, Delphine; and their daughter, Marcella. While living in the Sacramento apartment, their second child, Paul, was born, and they needed bigger quarters. There were many Victorian homes with beautiful architectural detail along tree-lined streets in the neighborhood around their apartment, but banks were not willing to finance loans for these homes. The reason for this denial was called redlining.

Redlining was created in 1933 by the Home Owners Loan Corporation, or HOLC, a federal program initiated to allow financing of home loans during the Great Depression. HOLC made mortgages commonplace and widely available, but they were not available to all or in all places. Their administrators developed a rating system that undervalued older, densely populated or mixed-use neighborhoods. Grouped into four colors—green, blue, yellow and red, from lowest risk to highest—neighborhoods were automatically assigned a higher risk if the buildings were old or poorly maintained or if their residents were nonwhite. HOLC's appraisal methods were adopted by the Federal Housing Administration, becoming part of the requirements to obtain an FHA home loan. Cities were surveyed by neighborhood to determine their suitability for home loans. In 1938, HOLC surveyed Sacramento, creating a color-coded map. Except for Poverty Ridge, rated blue, the entire Old City was rated yellow or red—high risk. Banks utilized redlining maps to assess mortgage risk even for non-FHA loans, and for the Old City, a mixed-use, mixed-race neighborhood of old buildings, loans were nearly impossible. Part of the justification for redevelopment of the old West End was elimination of the two main factors that redlined the neighborhood: the old buildings and their poor, nonwhite occupants. Laws against racial exclusion covenants and housing discrimination did not eliminate redlining because it discriminated against neighborhoods, not the person seeking housing.[74]

Investors could purchase homes if they had enough money to buy a home outright, or they could borrow against tangible assets like other real estate. But individual families rarely had those resources. Investors were often encouraged to demolish buildings using a method called "double-declining balance depreciation" that allowed investors to deduct the cost of demolishing a home on a property from its assessed value. "You'd see a house on a 40- by 160-[foot] house, with, say, a bungalow, and they'd say the value is $19,000 but the sale was $17,000 because you had demolition costs," said Delphine, "They put up the apartments and the investors made

Above: Home restorer Dennis Sorgen (left) and craftsman Rick Ball on the stairs of Rick's restored home at Twentieth and N Streets. *Center for Sacramento History,* Suttertown News *collection.*

Left: Bob, Eden, Jason and Roberta Rakela with Steven Ballew (left to right.) Bob and Steven founded High Rollers, a skate rental shop at Eighteenth and L Streets. *Center for Sacramento History,* Suttertown News *collection.*

money off the double declining balance." The properties that replaced the homes, including Italianate and Queen Anne homes or Craftsman bungalows, were often rectangular "dingbat" apartments, filling the entire lot with eight to sixteen apartments, or two-story "four-plex" apartments with shingled fronts.

Jim and Delphine searched in vain for a bank that would finance a home until they met Marjorie and Dick Munden. The Mundens had a house to sell at 2230 H Street, and Dick, an accountant, knew how to draw up a contract of sale. Instead of conventional financing, the Cathcarts paid the Mundens directly every month, eventually paying off the loan. At the end of the payment period, the Mundens signed the property directly over. This method, called "stuckee" financing, was little known, but it provided an alternative to conventional loans. "Stuckee" financing paid more than rent, and if the borrower defaulted, the owner retained the property. Once they had the house, the Cathcarts encountered another obstacle when they sought a building permit from city planning staff. Jim explained:

> We had dinner one night, and I fell through the floor! It was a very old floor, a brick foundation, and there wasn't much room between floor and foundation…so there was some dry rot there, and the best thing was to replace the foundation. So I went to get a building permit, and they told me, "You have to bring up the plumbing, the electrical, ad forty-two inch rails on the front porch—you have to build the entire house up to code"! I said, "Well, is there any way around it?" They said, "No," so I did it anyway. I did the whole thing according to code, and then I got red-tagged. And when we got red-tagged, we went down to city council during the public comment period after the meeting and said, "This is not acceptable! If you want to save housing Downtown, if you want to save your housing stock, if you want to save the history of Sacramento, you have to make an alternative historic building code."

The Cathcarts discovered that more families were in the same situation. They wanted to buy homes but could not finance them due to redlining. They wanted to restore the buildings but could not fix them due to city building codes. Some members of the Sacramento City Council were sympathetic, including those newly elected after the 1971 charter revision, but the building industry was very strong, organized and used to getting its way at city hall. In order to make their voices heard, neighborhood residents joined forces, forming the Sacramento Old City Association in 1972. The

Cathcarts and the Mundens met other advocates, including Bill Atherton and Steve and Susan Larson. Susan became one of SOCA's earliest leaders and helped secure the organization's reputation for relentless advocacy.[75]

SUSAN LARSON: BUTTING HEADS WITH DEVELOPERS

In 1970, Susan Larson and her husband, Steve, moved to Sacramento, where they, like the Cathcarts, fell in love with the residential architecture, the tree-lined streets and the proximity to Steve's job at the state capitol. They were equally disturbed by the rapid demolition occurring in the neighborhood and the barriers to restoring buildings by homeowners. Larson focused her efforts on the biggest developers, Bardeis & Rynan:

Bardeis and Rynan were tearing down hundreds and hundreds of buildings…they are the ones that built all of those fourplexes that are everywhere in Midtown. We had some real problems with the general plan and the fact that the city envisioned all of Midtown [as] high-density residential, R5. The city's view was this is a slum, we're going to tear it all down, we're going to build nothing but apartment houses and it's going to look like a giant hairbrush! We got together to fight for preservation…I had access to a mimeograph machine, so I was the editor of this newsletter, it was sort of like Susan's stream of consciousness, and I called it the Doily Cart.

So we met every month, had agendas, and we pulled people to us. My husband worked in the legislature; we had several people who were legislative consultants who were specialists. Fred Silva, [a] masterful land use specialist, was a consultant over there. Steve Taber, absolutely a brilliant guy. He was a lawyer…We had all these people that were professional people, working in the legislature, so we knew exactly how to do things. We printed up reports like there was no tomorrow on land use and traffic—the specialist on land use was Fred, and the specialist on traffic was Steve—so we had position papers. SOCA may have started as a very small little group, we were all doing sweat equity in our houses. None of us could afford a contractor. We did a lot of our own work; it was just sort of the way things were. We had a lot of professionally drafted position papers about the planning issues that the city of Sacramento needed to face, and we testified constantly!

Redlining, zoning and building codes made buildings like this Colonial Revival mansion at Eighteenth and N Streets easier to demolish than repair. Protected as a historic building, it was restored a few years after this photo was taken in 2005. *Photo by author.*

By 1975, Susan became president of SOCA and frequently served as the public face of the organization. Mary Helmich and Steve Taber took over the newsletter, renaming it the *Old City Guardian*. While the Cathcarts focused their efforts on lending policies, the Larsons engaged in public and private dialogues with the real estate developers that replaced Victorian homes with inexpensive fourplex apartments. Susan described her confrontational relationship with developer Chris Bardies:

> *I testified a lot at the City Council and the Planning Commission and everywhere else, and was the old house freak, basically. And the face they saw a lot was me, and Chris Bardeis was the face for Bardeis & Rynan. And basically every single week, I was complaining about what Chris was doing, and he was complaining that I was a complete insane nut. In those days, the way the council chambers were set up, it was much more intimate…the media was there, the council people were accessible, the council office was just right off the chamber and you walked right by it to*

get to the chamber. And everybody was always talking out in the hall. So Chris and I would be talking outside, waiting for our item to come up, and we were perfectly friendly outside the chambers. We'd go in the chambers, and he'd call me names, I'd call him names. But Chris, I believe, recognized after a few years of this that the tide was changing. The city had decided to get a little bit on board, there was preservation research going on…he kind of saw that it was getting harder and harder to tear down these buildings and the city was going to step in.

After years of butting heads at city council meetings, the two formed an unlikely partnership in 1975 to protect the Dunn Mansion, a dramatic 1900 Colonial Revival home constructed for attorney Chauncey L. Dunn, located at 2219 Capitol Avenue. Next door to the Dunn Mansion was a Baptist church, which owned the property and hoped to demolish it in order to create a parking lot for its congregation. SOCA members objected to the demolition, bringing the matter to the city council's attention. The church claimed that demolition was necessary because nobody wanted to buy the house, so Jim Cathcart submitted a formal bid to purchase the building. Once the sale was approved, the Cathcarts planned to move the house, but city regulations made house relocation nearly impossible. Larson described the final resolution:

Several people had tried, and the city was not at all cooperative about moving the buildings off the land that somebody wanted into a place where they could be remodeled. And the city building department came up with every reason under the sun that you couldn't allow a building to be moved…Chris moved the Dunn Mansion—that was his last Midtown project, he actually saved a significant building. And he was the only one who could have done it because he knew everybody in the building department he was so active a builder in Midtown. So there wasn't anybody he didn't know…Chris tipped his hat to all of us and said, "I'm going to leave Midtown, but I'm going to do something really good." And so I am very grateful to him, but a lot of it was because he and I did talk all the time, and I was perfectly friendly when we were in private. I only called him names in public!

On July 31, 1975, the Sacramento City Council approved relocation of the Dunn Mansion and asked city staff to develop a policy to facilitate relocation of historic buildings. The Dunn Mansion was relocated to 2129 L Street, where it remains today, marked with a plaque to commemorate its survival.[76]

VANISHING VICTORIANS

Many Sacramentans consider the demolition of the Alhambra Theatre in 1973 the catalyst for Sacramento's historic preservation program, but for members of SOCA, the primary issue was demolition of housing in the central city, a process already underway before the closure and demolition of the Alhambra. Historic preservation meant more than the city's grandest architectural landmarks, historic sites like Old Sacramento or commercial buildings like the Alhambra. The old neighborhoods, with their eclectic architectural character, represented more than the sum of their parts when considered as a whole. Even in their dilapidated state, interspersed with new apartments and old vacant lots, the rhythm of the buildings from the street created a sense of place, with different parts of the city representing unique eras of construction. Other than limited identification of a handful of historic West End buildings during the creation of Old Sacramento, no systematic survey of the Old City's residential architecture existed. That changed in 1973 with the publishing of *Vanishing Victorians* by the American Association of University Women.

Organized and primarily researched by architectural historian Paula Boghosian, *Vanishing Victorians* divided the architecture of the Old City into nine neighborhoods, each with its own general boundary and context. Homes of the Victorian era, generally the 1850s until the early 1900s, were emphasized, including Italianate, Second Empire, Stick, Shingle and Queen Anne styles. A final chapter included individual properties not located in the nine designated areas, and an addendum included "Vanished Victorians" of note that had already fallen. Boghosian's approach was inclusive and diverse. Basing homes' inclusion on a common architectural and social legacy, she listed dramatic, architect-designed homes—such as the Heilbron, Crocker, Hale, Stanford and Gallatin mansions—alongside the modest homes of clerks and railroad employees. The book provided an accessible way to appreciate Sacramento's residential architecture and included foldout maps of self-guided tours so those on foot, bicycle or automobile could explore these neighborhoods firsthand.[77]

The year 1973 also inaugurated the first SOCA bicycle tours. Held in late summer or early fall, these tours were group recreational rides covering several miles, with each year having a different route. The rides went past notable architectural landmarks and restoration projects in progress, ending with a picnic in a city park. Bicycles helped riders move between homes that were dispersed throughout the entire Old City, too far for a comfortable walk.

SOCA was involved in efforts to save the Llewellyn Williams mansion at Tenth and H Streets. *Photo by Joe Perfecto.*

On "Bike to Work Day," cycling activists advocated safer cycling routes and alternatives to smog-producing auto traffic. *Photo by Joe Perfecto.*

The Rakela family restored this Queen Anne home on Twentieth Street, featured in several of SOCA's historic home tours. *Photo courtesy of Mickey Abbey.*

The ride also served as a social event, as SOCA also existed to serve a social function, bringing together people of similar interests for mutual support. Advocacy and research was key to achieving their organizational goals, but fun was essential to keep members engaged. Seeing projects underway also helped inspire others to pursue their own rehab and restoration projects.

In 1974, SOCA gave visitors an even closer look at their historic homes with the first Old City Home Tour. This event served a dual role, as a fundraiser to pursue the group's objectives and a marketing tool to show people what could be accomplished. These tours allowed visitors to enter each house and see firsthand the workmanship of the old homes and the craftsmanship of their new owners. These marketing efforts and advocacy at city hall were sufficient to convince the city to perform a more detailed survey of Old City architecture in 1975, which was conducted by the architectural consulting firm of Charles Hall Page. This survey documented the residential areas of the Old City, including properties built in the early 1920s. In 1975, the City of Sacramento passed its first historic preservation ordinance. Included in the new ordinance was an alternative building code to allow easier rehabilitation of historic buildings. A new Preservation Commission was formed with historian Paula Boghosian. In 1976, a year when the nation's bicentennial brought enormous interest to local historic preservation efforts, the Charles Hall Page survey was adopted to create the city's first official register of historic buildings. This survey set the stage for later surveys that included nonresidential buildings and allowed the creation of new historic landmarks and districts. Redlining slowly declined as banks were convinced to lend, and the Community Reinvestment Act of 1977 reduced discriminatory credit practices against low-income neighborhoods.

RESISTING DEMOLITION AND GENTRIFICATION

The preservation ordinance represented a limited amount of protection for city landmarks, but many in the real estate community and city government were not convinced that the Old City was a suitable place to live. Dale Kooyman, an Iowa native who moved to California in 1958, received advice about Downtown Sacramento prior to relocating from the Bay Area to Sacramento for a job:

> *I was told when I got the job here by a high official in San Francisco, "You're not going to like it in Sacramento. You've lived in Chicago, you've lived in LA, you lived all these places and you're not going to like it. It's got a beautiful residential area but it's all going to be torn down, you don't want to live there."*

After arriving in Sacramento, Dale found a property for sale at Twenty-first and H Streets. He appreciated the beautiful Art Deco furnishings of the home, the Arts and Crafts architecture of nearby Boulevard Park, the coffee shop across the street, the short walk to work and even the convenient laundromat on the corner. His real estate agent recommended the neighborhood for its investment potential, not the value of what was there:

> *He said, you're so lucky to get this, because…East Sacramento is way pricier than you want to pay, and you can't walk to Downtown. And that's what I wanted to do—I wanted to live in an area where I could walk straight Downtown. Even though I knew I was going to be traveling a lot,*

I wanted to walk Downtown, morning, night, through the capitol, through the neighborhoods, because I really liked the scenery!...He said the reason is that, all this area, those old houses aren't worth saving...And that's when he told me the whole area was planned to be destroyed for low-income housing. And businesses will be along Nineteenth, Twenty-first, J and L Street[s]. And I thought at the time, if these are going to be low-income, who is going to patronize those businesses and offices?...Then he explained in detail that those streets being office and J, K and L being office, retail and businesses, you can sell your property for twice as much because down here will be attorneys and doctors. I said, well, okay, but I still could not believe that the city would do such a thing, because being from the Midwest, and having traveled in the East and the South, it was these kinds of houses that were in the upper [class] *neighborhoods!*

Dale avoided redlining by borrowing against property he owned in Santa Cruz. Despite his realtor's prediction, the wave of demolition slowed and then stopped, followed by a slow wave of rehabilitation as formerly dilapidated homes were purchased by a growing number of people drawn to the Old City. With new residents came pressure on police to curb neighborhood issues including prostitution, drug dealing and high-speed traffic during commute hours. New neighborhood associations formed within the Old City, focusing on more neighborhood-specific issues. Some attended meetings or lobbied the city, while others, like Paul Harriman, simply swept up trash and leaves on the block near his I Street home. His example encouraged others to do the same, making a drug dealer who worked on Harriman's block so uncomfortable that he moved to a different neighborhood.[78] In the historic districts, the value of land went down, less viable for new construction, but the value of the houses grew, as they were recognized for their value as something other than an obstacle to be demolished. What was previously viewed as obsolescence became part of their curb appeal.[79]

In 1978, graduate student Robin Datel conducted a survey of SOCA members. Most were in their twenties and thirties, and about half were married, some with young children. Two-thirds of those living in the Old City also worked there. They were generally white and well-educated, middle-class and often recent arrivals in Sacramento. The most important considerations that drew them to the Old City were the beauty of the older homes and their majestic tree cover. They liked the proximity to work and amenities, its central location and the reduced dependency on an automobile, but they were driven by love for old houses. If the City of Sacramento did

Neighborhood activist protesters urge commuters to slow down on P Street, July 1975. *Center for Sacramento History,* Sacramento Bee *collection.*

not see the potential of those homes, SOCA members certainly did and worked to raise public awareness of their value.

Many SOCA members were newcomers to Sacramento, but some longtime residents with pride in their historic homes joined, including social worker and artist Socorro Zuniga, who joined in 1977. She chose her home in the Washington neighborhood in 1953, a 1905 Wright & Kimbrough bungalow, to remain close to her family and Sacramento's Latino community and because she appreciated its architectural grandeur. SOCA members valued the social and economic diversity of the Old City and were strongly influenced by Jane Jacobs's principles of walkability, including the fine-grained mixtures of land uses and diversity of population that were traditional to the Old City but unknown in suburban tracts. Gentrification and displacement of existing population was seen as an undesirable but sometimes unavoidable consequence of their activities but as far less damaging to the city or harmful to people than the mass displacements of redevelopment. Demolition of the West End and loss of Downtown housing meant that, by the early 1970s, there were relatively few people to displace.[80] Susan Larson commented, "Most of us didn't displace very many people, and you needed gentrification. Are there some negative side effects? Of course there are, but at the same time, you have to look at where the balance is. I think that it was better not to lose nine hundred square blocks, and that's really what it was all about."

SOCA members tried to limit the effects of their own projects by relocating existing tenants. When the Cathcarts purchased an Italianate mansion at Nineteenth and N Streets, it was divided into eleven apartments, each inhabited by an elderly man. Before restoring the building, Delphine gradually moved the tenants into nearby apartment buildings over the next three years, rather than evict them all. "It was the more humane way to do it," said Jim. As the business community noticed Midtown's growth, they often took a less delicate approach.[81]

SAVING DOWNTOWN HOUSING:
THE FRANCESCA AND THE MERRIUM

By the early 1980s, SOCA had more than five hundred members. With the end of redlining and the beginning of historic preservation, the organization turned its attention to the central business district. Two major battles were over a pair of midrise apartment buildings, the Merrium and the Francesca. The five-story, forty-one-apartment Merrium at Fourteenth and K Streets was built in 1912 and designed in the Prairie style with a broad, overhanging cornice. The Francesca at Thirteenth and L Streets was a six-story Spanish Colonial Revival building across the street from Capitol Park. On the Francesca's ground floor was David's Brass Rail, a politicians' bar and a favorite of Jerry Brown. Both were reasonably priced but more expensive than Downtown SRO hotels, and unlike SRO units, they were self-contained apartments with kitchens and bathrooms. Their proximity to the capital attracted young lobbyists and junior legislative aides who valued their closeness to work and classic architectural style. Their low rent also attracted creative people like Gerald Zarrilli, a writer who lived at the Francesca and worked part-time at the Country Maid restaurant. "It reminds me of the buildings back East, where I'm from," said Zarrilli. "I can sit at my typewriter and look out at the dome as an excuse not to write."

In 1983, a twenty-story high-rise office and twelve-story hotel were proposed for the Francesca's site. The property was previously listed as a city landmark but was delisted in June 1982 when the landmark list was revised. An economic slowdown stalled the project, but in 1984, the properties adjacent to the Francesca were sold, leaving the Francesca under separate ownership. From that year until 1987, the Hyatt Regency Hotel was constructed behind and around the Merrium, until developer Gregg Lukenbill pushed to acquire and demolish the building, claiming it was an eyesore obstructing

David's Brass Rail, across L Street from the capitol, was a popular politicians' bar on the ground floor of the Francesca Apartments. *Center for Sacramento History,* Suttertown News *collection.*

The Francesca Apartments were demolished, at the cost of affordable downtown housing, because they obstructed hotel visitors' view of Capitol Park. *Center for Sacramento History,* Suttertown News *collection.*

Three young residents of the Merrium Apartments protest its planned demolition in October 1988. *Center for Sacramento History,* Suttertown News *collection.*

his view of Capitol Park. In 1988, a San Francisco hotelier who tried to buy the property was rebuffed. The building was demolished in September and October 1988, replaced by a landscaped plaza.

Just as the wrecking ball descended on the Francesca, the Merrium faced an expansion of the Sacramento Convention Center. Blocked from expansion to the north, south or west by the Community Center Theater and planned high-rise towers, the natural direction for expansion was eastward, requiring demolition of a city block that included Beers Books and the Merrium Apartments. The building's owners, Hank Fisher and Ray Stone, considered the loss of housing inconsequential, comparing it to blowing a speck of dust off a desk. As with the Francesca, the Merrium's residents preferred proximity to Downtown, including Elaine Hamby, who said, "Not everyone wants to join the rush to the suburbs at the close of the working day." SOCA filed a lawsuit against the city in December 1988, hoping to block demolition and retain the urban housing. The lawsuit stretched over three years, but in September 1991, the Merrium fell. *Suttertown News* editor Tim Holt summarized the loss of the Merrium and Francesca, along with the Californian Hotel, a residential hotel on Eighth and I Streets:

> [T]*he three former residences shown on this page were torn down by the city itself, a city whose leaders give lip service to the "24-hour city" concept, but whose actions indicate they're still mired in the redevelopment mentality of the '50s—rip up the fabric of urban life (small business, affordable housing) to put up Big, Dazzling Buildings (the Hyatt, the new Central Library, the Convention Center). The bulldozer mentality evidenced on this page raises a very fundamental question: Just whose side is City Hall on, anyway? Certainly not on the side of the Francesca's residents, who were forced to move because they were blocking the scenic views of their higher-rent neighbors in the Hyatt Hotel. After all, the city had already poured taxpayer subsidies into the Hyatt, so this was just a way of protecting the city's investment. Indeed, it seems the city regards conventioneers and other out-of-town visitors as a more important constituency than the city's residents.*[82]

SOCA was involved in many other efforts to protect and restore historic landmarks within the boundaries of the Old City, including the Memorial Auditorium and the Llewellyn Williams Mansion, but retaining housing in order to ensure the viability and diversity of neighborhoods was its highest priority. Developers still considered the Old City unsuitable for ownership housing, and while SOCA had friends on the council, others, like Midtown resident David Shore, were less friendly to preservation. Shore even earned the nickname "Demolition Dave" after his votes to demolish the Francesca and Merrium.[83] If new construction was a numbers game involving real estate dollars for developers and tax dollars for city government, the numbers that mattered most for SOCA and Midtown residents were population figures.

SOCA members attend the 1994 "Fainted Ladies" tour, a bus tour of Old City homes in poor repair intended to highlight landlords unwilling to maintain their properties, led by Karen Jacques. *Photo by Joe Perfecto.*

Infill housing started to rise on former vacant lots, and dilapidated mansions received long-deferred attention. In 1994, Robin Datel reexamined the Old City, asking if gentrification had destroyed the diversity that was important to SOCA members, and found that it had not. Despite dramatically increased property values and greater population, a high proportion of affordable housing stood alongside restored historic homes, with rents that were lower than the county average. Ethnic diversity actually increased, at a higher rate than the city as a whole. Despite demolition, census figures between 1970 and 1990 represented the first rise in Old City population in decades, growing from 27,205 to 31,648. An anonymous response to Datel's survey summed up the Old City in three words: "Diversity. Trees. Coffee."

Datel suggested several explanations for this gentler form of gentrification. Sacramento's outward suburban growth meant there was less unmet demand for housing. Developers were mostly uninterested in building new for-sale housing in the Old City, considering offices more profitable.[84] The diversity of Midtown's built environment, with 85 percent of Old City blocks featuring both commercial and residential uses, differed from the consistent pattern of many gentrified older neighborhoods. The "dingbat" apartments and fourplexes, the bane of early preservationists, moderated the effects of gentrification by supplying affordable housing. Preservationists restored old Victorian homes from rooming houses to single-family homes alongside the newer apartment buildings, mixing low-income renters with middle-class homeowners. Because diversity was a priority for SOCA members, they worked to preserve affordable housing, not just mansions and architectural landmarks, as seen in the fights to save the Merrium and Francesca. In the 1980s, a new generation followed the baby boomers into Midtown. They could not afford to buy the historic homes, but thanks to those inexpensive apartments, they could live in the same neighborhood.[85]

6

Slouching Toward Midtown

Sacramento, the convalescent home of California, a state worker's suburban playground, retirement city for the middle class military mind. Deep in the Downtown district, as night descends on the blemish of the valley and the tailor-fitted suburbanites escape to their 19" color TV, five oddly-dressed young men, smelling like a cross between a brewery and a barrel full of soiled socks, come noisily staggering out of the damp alley, belching and mumbling incoherent babble. At first glance, one might mistake them as a brigade of winos or a flock of shopping cart men. But no! It's Sacto's masters of musical mischief, the TALES OF TERROR. Having settled back home after an overextended, financially disastrous tour of the U.S. of A., these 5 freaks of nature are doing what they do best…playing music, drinking, and passing out. In other words, having a blast.
—Scott Soriano[86]

Joan Didion's "Slouching Towards Bethlehem" gave a grim assessment of baby boom counterculture. Named after a line from the William Butler Yeats poem "The Second Coming," a dark vision of the Antichrist's approach, Didion's gin- and amphetamine-fueled essay used horrific imagery to capture the less glamorous elements of hippie life: "All that seemed clear was that at some point we had aborted ourselves and butchered the job, and because nothing else seemed so relevant I decided to go to San Francisco. San Francisco was where the social hemorrhaging was showing up. San Francisco was where the missing children were gathering and calling themselves 'hippies.'"[87]

The subsequent countercultural expressions of Generation X led with the horror, brutal imagery and bleak, alienated outlook that Didion found

The Ramones at El Dorado Saloon on September 14, 1986, a Clear and Distinct Ideas show. (Stewart Katz is in baseball cap on the right.) The Ramones played the first punk show in Sacramento in 1977. *Photo by John Muheim.*

beneath the paisley surface of the Love Generation. Embracing shock value and nihilism, punk rejected the broken promises of the hippies but shared their dissatisfaction with the suburban lifestyle. "All You Need Is Love" became "Let's Have a War," and teenagers with shaved heads could not wear flowers in their hair. In many ways, this surface of aggression was protective camouflage that kept an alienating world at bay. Beneath its angry surface, punk was about liberation and expression. Punks followed hippies to the Old City, seeking community and acceptance, places of congregation and artistic expression and cheap rent.

Punk emerged from cities like London and New York in the mid-1970s, rapidly spreading to smaller cities. In Manchester, England, postpunk bands united around Factory Records, operating outside the traditional major-label apparatus and the London social scene. When suburban high school kids from Washington, D.C., visited New York punk venues in the late 1970s, they were called "muscleheads" by the more artistically inclined members of the New York punk scene, including rock critic Lester Bangs. Young D.C. punks like Ian Mackaye (lead singer of Minor Threat and Fugazi) turned the

Lorna Clark in the Club Minimal office. *Photo by John Muheim.*

phrase around, assuming that a musclehead was someone with a very strong brain. Mackaye's record label Dischord Records released an influential compilation album named *Flex Your Head* as another jab at the "musclehead" trope. Mackaye's first experience with punk was a January 1979 benefit show featuring the Cramps, a legendary punk band founded by Lux Interior and Poison Ivy. Lux (aka Eric Purkheiser) and Ivy (aka Kristy Wallace) met while attending Sacramento State and started record collecting on K Street in the early 1970s before moving to Ohio and later New York City to form the Cramps.[88] According to Dennis Yudt, Sacramento's first punk show was an August 1976 show at Slick Willie's, featuring the Ramones. As in other cities across the United States, audiences, inspired by punk's accessibility and tired of mainstream rock's overproduced and indulgent inaccessibility, were inspired to start their own bands.[89]

PUNK PIONEERS: OZZIE AND THE TWINKEYZ

Sacramento's rock music scene was in rough shape in the 1970s. Efforts to restrain teenage abandon continued under John Misterly's successor, Sheriff Duane Lowe, and the sheriff's counterparts in the city police department, limiting the number of live rock venues. Small clubs and bars were primarily interested in cover bands. KZAP continued its dominance of local airwaves, along with its competitors KROY and Earth Radio, but focused more on major-label hits than earlier free-form experiments. Two bands, Ozzie and the Twinkeyz, sprung from this moribund era. Neither fit the later stereotype of a punk band, but both set the tone for rock music outside the mainstream.

Ozzie began in 1971 as a jam session among Sacramento State students William Fuller, Spencer Sparrow and Jack Hastings. All volunteered at the student-run KERS radio station and shared a love of Captain Beefheart. Originally forming as the Reds, White and Blues, or RWB, they played free-form sets with as many as twelve members, including Greg "the Charmer" Chargin and Bob Jolly. They practiced at Sparrow's Midtown apartment on Twenty-third and N Streets. Their only live show was at DeWitt State Hospital, a mental health facility in a decommissioned army base near Auburn. After the DeWitt show, they decided to pursue a more traditional song-centric approach, and a more accessible name, Girl Fight, in 1973.

For Girl Fight, accessibility was a matter of degree, playing songs by the Velvet Underground and the Electric Prunes instead of Top 40 hits. The

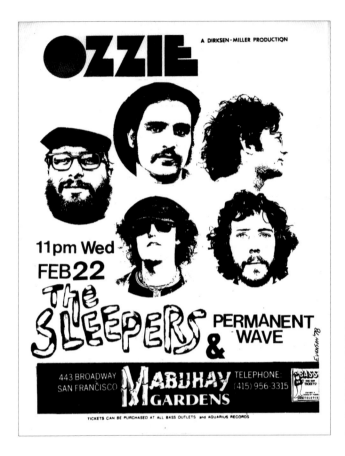

Flyer for Ozzie show at Mabuhay Gardens, San Francisco, circa 1979. Ozzie shared the bill with fellow Sacramento New Wave band Permanent Wave. *Image courtesy of Dane Henas.*

manager of Campus Pizza booked Girl Fight because he considered them so unlistenable they would scare off the bar's regulars, a group of rowdy bikers. Despite his expectation, the bikers loved Girl Fight, and the bar manager offered them a regular weekly gig.

When a new restaurant, the Great Northern Food and Beverage Company, opened in Sacramento, Fuller applied for a job. All the hosts, bus staff and waiters were musicians, expected to perform live music at the restaurant in addition to their regular duties, so Great Northern became a hub for local musicians. Fuller met their future keyboard player Gary Sears and their future manager Bo Richards while working there. After a failed effort to secure a major-label record deal, Girl Fight replaced drummer Greg Chargin with Bob Jolly's brother David and renamed themselves Ozzie, inspired by 1950s TV star and bandleader Ozzie Nelson. In 1973, the band's rehearsal space moved to Pigeon Manor, a Victorian home at Twenty-first and P, where

Sears, Jolly and Bo Richards also lived. Drummer Lenny Schotter replaced Jolly on drums in 1975. Their musical directions were influenced by Roxy Music, David Bowie, and English progressive rock.

In 1977, Ozzie recorded their first single at David Houston's Moon Studios. Houston saw a kindred spirit in Ozzie, and the band liked the do-it-yourself spirit of his recording studio. Record production was equally do-it-yourself, with the members of the band hand-cutting thousands of record sleeves and stuffing them with records. Their first single, "Android Love," was released on Bo Richards's Make Me Records label, with airplay on KZAP and other northern California radio stations. Their other releases included provocative titles like "Child of the Reich" and "Your Love Is Like a Gas Chamber." Ozzie became regulars at pioneering San Francisco punk venue Mabuhay Gardens, supporting San Francisco punk bands—including the Nuns, the Avengers and the Mutants—and fellow Sacramento bands like Permanent Wave. In Sacramento, the band played supporting gigs with touring bands, including the Talking Heads and the Nerves. In 1978, Ozzie contributed a rock opera, "Berlin 1990," to KZAP's tenth anniversary celebration; the opera was the tale of a postnuclear world in which the city of Berlin was the last outpost of human life. By this time, record labels were marketing the more accessible (and least self-destructive) acts from the punk scene, including Blondie, Devo and the Talking Heads, as "New Wave." Bands like Ozzie adopted the "New Wave" moniker as a middle ground between punk alienation and mainstream rock's commercial potential, becoming part of a larger Sacramento New Wave scene that included Permanent Wave (later reformed as the Mumbles), Alternative Learning, Labial Fricative and the Suspects.

In May 1980, Ozzie moved to Los Angeles, feeling that it had plateaued in Sacramento, but found limited success. In 1982, representatives of heavy metal singer Ozzy Osbourne's record label asked the band to change its name. An offer by the band to compete for rights to the name via a tag-team wrestling match was rejected, so Ozzie renamed itself "Anonymo" to avoid a lawsuit. After playing a few gigs under the new name, the band broke up, and its members went their separate ways.[90]

The Twinkeyz were the musical brainchild of Sacramento native Donnie Jupiter. Raised in South Sacramento, Donnie (born Don Marquez in 1949) had a lifelong interest in science fiction and music. As a teenager, he attended live shows at the Home Front and visited Jodette's Failasouf Shop. His own music was influenced by Lou Reed and T. Rex, and he was in the audience when the Ramones first played Slick Willie's. In 1977, Donnie joined forces with Walter Smith, Tom Darling and Steve Bateman to form

The Twinkeyz, pioneers of Sacramento punk, at the Funland arcade, Twelfth and J Streets. *Photo by Dane Henas.*

the Twinkeyz. According to Jupiter, "Any other bands before that never got beyond just sitting around and rehearsing. I was mainly a record collector; the other people in the band were also record collectors. We weren't really happy with the new music that was coming out at the time and figured we could do better on our own."

The Twinkeyz shared some of the same prog-rock influences as Ozzie, but instead of Ozzie's ironic and satirical attitude, the Twinkeyz had a lighter and more humorous tone, incorporating their interest in comics and science fiction. They still maintained an alienated perspective about the world around them, best characterized in their single, "Aliens in Our Midst," about which, Jupiter noted, "I wanted it to be about aliens, literally, but just alienation also. There is always a science fiction theme to my music and lyrics. It seems that only a few people really fit into society that well. Maybe I exaggerate my own misfit nature, I suppose I always felt that way a little bit." They also followed Ozzie's lead and recorded their songs at David Houston's Moon Studios.

The band released three singles and played fewer than ten gigs before breaking up in 1980. Donnie opened a record shop on K Street in 1978, Markee Records, but was not satisfied with the potential of Sacramento's live music scene, or the relationship of city government and officials with rock musicians and even record stores:

I think there never really got to be much of a youth culture in Sacramento. I just don't think it was ever cultivated here. Teenagers can't go rent halls on their own, there has to be some kind of adult input and nurturing to go on for that to happen. Just like the Home Front, in the church, someone to put those gigs on…It never really seemed like there was that much going on. The record store that I ran, and the comic book store that I worked at, both businesses at one time or another had somebody, either a cop or another business owner, who thought we were dealing drugs out of there. Just because they couldn't figure out why or how a comic book store or a record store could do business—there had to be something going on. There was just always a bit [of an] askance view, you know…Sacramento is not a place you come to, to make the big time in show business.

Donnie ran Markee Records on K Street well into the 1980s and joined another punk band, the Lizards, formed by comic book store owner and musician Dave Downey. While they played fewer gigs than Ozzie and did not endure as long, they both influenced later Sacramento punk bands.

SKATING IN RANCHO CORDOVA

When Dennis Yudt arrived in Rancho Cordova, he experienced a serious culture shock. Growing up in an air force family, his junior high school in Cheyenne, Wyoming, had a graduating class of four people. His father was stationed at Mather Air Force Base as a dietitian in 1977, moving Dennis to Rancho Cordova, where he attended Mitchell Junior High School and Cordova High and felt like a fish out of water. According to Yudt, "I tried to fit in. I would see Led Zeppelin T-shirts or KZAP T-shirts. I tried to assimilate myself to youth culture of the day, but I was just a nerdy Eurasian kid, still wearing Toughskins jeans and plaid shirts."

Dennis discovered two elements of teenage Rancho Cordova life in which he could participate, music and skateboarding. The music was the heavy metal and arena rock of KZAP, and skateboarding was just starting its second wave of late 1970s popularity. The Sierra Wave Skate Park in Rosemont was a popular spot for Rancho Cordova skaters, but skate crews like the N-Men preferred less controlled environments, including concrete culverts, drainage ditches, parking structures and construction sites. K Street Mall's concrete sculptures and hard surfaces were unpopular with residents and visitors but became a skater's paradise. Northern California skaters developed an all-terrain style, based on the rough concrete environments where they grew up. While any

The RC Boys at Kin's Coloma, circa 1981. *Left to right*: Dennis Yudt, John "Stamo" Stamotellos, Pat "Rat's Ass" Stratford and Bob "Elmo" Ellsworth. Not pictured is Dave Perry on rhythm guitar. *Photo courtesy of Jerry Perry.*

empty pool became a potential pirate skating spot, based on the inspiration of Southern California skaters, northern California skaters eschewed the fluid, surfer-inspired Southern California style for a more aggressive approach.

If Southern California's long-haired surfers were anathema to northern California skaters, so were long-haired heavy metal bands as soon as the rough-edged and close-cropped fashions of punk arrived. As Dennis Yudt described it, "When we saw Devo, all the Rancho Cordova skaters cut their hair off." Many of the skaters also became more actively involved in music. Some became fans, while others formed their own bands. Dennis joined forces with a classmate, drummer Pat Stratford, along with Bob "Elmo" Ellsworth on bass, John "Stamo" Stamotellos playing lead guitar and Dave Perry on rhythm guitar. They named themselves the RC Boys, nominally standing for Rancho Cordova, or "Rad Conspiracy." Finding a venue was a challenge, as Rancho Cordova was a small suburb with few live music options, especially for teenagers. Perry convinced the owner of a Chinese restaurant on Folsom Boulevard, Kin's Coloma, to host punk shows in early 1981. The owner agreed, hoping to sell dinners to those attending shows. Shows continued at Kin's until early 1982, with a young promoter named Jerry Perry taking over Dave Perry's role as show organizer. The RC Boys were the opening act for most of the Kin's Coloma shows. At least one show, featuring headliner 7 Seconds from Reno, was shut down by police. Undaunted, someone offered to continue the show in their backyard, so 7 Seconds played around their swimming pool, an experience that left a positive impression of the adaptable, creative Sacramento punks on the band's lead singer. The RC Boys broke up in 1982, shortly after the end of the Kin's Coloma shows. Pat Stratford traded his drums to sing for a new band, the Square Cools.[91]

Do It Yourself in Midtown

Part of punk's appeal to alienated youth was its accessibility. Major record labels promoted rock stars as unapproachable idols with skills and talent beyond mortal ability, separated on dramatic arena stages where fans worshipped rock gods from a distance. Punks had no respect for major-label idolatry. Anyone could be in a band. Any building could be a punk venue. The only rule was "Do It Yourself." This aesthetic encouraged participation and creation of music, media, fashion and community. In the age before the Internet, bands with no management or record label toured via friends in neighboring cities. An informal infrastructure of music venues, coffee shops and record stores became outposts for underground music. Events were promoted by hand-distributed flyers, posters stapled to telephone poles or pinned onto bulletin boards and word of mouth. Photocopied, self-produced "'zines" shared opinions, band interviews and reports across a tenuous national network. Sacramento's role in this network drew kids to Midtown from suburban enclaves and small towns. The official city reaction to punk venues varied between disdain and open hostility, but this community demonstrated sufficient strength to stand up for their rights.

Punk epicenters typically formed in places where there were a sufficient number of alienated young people, and Sacramento's suburbs produced those in great quantity. Cheap rent and places to congregate, as with the art community, were critical. The San Francisco punk scene evolved around marginal spaces a decade too late for the Summer of Love. One such space was Filipino restaurant Mabuhay Gardens, sometimes described as the West Coast's equivalent of CBGB. Los Angeles had no shortage of live music venues and urban decay, helping overcome the city's lack of population density, but punk bands had difficulty booking traditional music venues, and underage kids had limited access to nightclubs. Because Sacramento's efforts

Skaters (left to right) Whirly Willy, Omar Rebee Snap, Jimmy the Snake, Mickey the Muscle, Tommy Checkers and Bill outside High Rollers skate shop at Eighteenth and L Streets, circa 1985. *Photo courtesy of Mickey Abbey.*

were focused on Downtown redevelopment zones and suburban growth, Midtown was generally ignored. When neighborhood activists forced prostitutes out of the Southside Park neighborhood in 1981, they relocated to a new crawl along Seventeenth Street. Until the 1950s, K Street between Fifteenth and Nineteenth Streets was Sacramento's "Auto Row," with many new and used car dealers. By the 1970s most were closed, resulting in a high rate of commercial vacancy, allowing prostitutes and johns to carry out their activities unobserved.[92] At Nineteenth and J Streets, a card room called Georgian's Casino had a notorious reputation as a prostitutes' bar and haven of drug dealers, who also worked on Midtown streets.[93] A haven for gambling, Georgian's also became a base of operations for local boxing promoters, including a young Sacramentan named Stewart Katz.

STEWART KATZ AND CLUB MINIMAL

Born in New York in 1955, Stewart arrived in Sacramento's Wilhaggin neighborhood about 1970. He got his start promoting events while a student at Sacramento State, drumming up interest for the college chess team, "Katz's Kamikazes," with team T-shirts, banners and a parade. Katz loved boxing but lacked the skill to make it as a professional fighter, so he became a boxing promoter at age twenty-two, the youngest in the city's history. He built a working relationship with boxing manager Karnak "Pidge" Georgian, whose family owned Sacramento bars and restaurants dating back to the days of the Equipoise Café at Fourth and K Streets in the old West End. In 1970, Georgian opened a card room and bar at Nineteenth and J Streets, and in the late 1970s, Georgian's Casino became Katz's base of operations.[94] Katz was also interested in music, especially punk. Using the skills he learned promoting boxing matches, Katz booked shows at places like the Odd Fellows Hall at Ninth and K, VFW Post 61 at Fifteenth and H, outer space–themed disco Galactica 2000 at Fifteenth and K and city-owned Clunie Hall in McKinley Park. He named his booking company "Clear and Distinct Ideas," or CDI.

Katz continued booking shows as an independent promoter but chafed at the limitations of using other people's venues. La Semilla Cultural Center, an office for leftist political organizations on Twentieth and C Streets, hosted punk shows until a bathroom wall was damaged during a show. CDI shows were often financially successful, drawing capacity crowds, but they strained relationships with venue owners and received official pressure from police, who were uncomfortable with the punk scene. According to scene veteran Scott Soriano, "Cops thought we were crazy people—their only exposure to our scene was the punk episode of *Quincy*." In June 1983, Katz leased a cinderblock garage in an industrial part of Curtis Park, 3747 West Pacific Avenue, owned by Katz's boxing associate Karnak Georgian, and named it Club Minimal.

Club Minimal had bare walls and few furnishings to minimize damage by rowdy punks. Visitors were welcome to tag graffiti inside the building, but defacing the exterior was forbidden, enforced by security staff made up of local punks, including Moose and Johnny No Style. The club was all-ages and had no liquor license. Club Minimal became a target of police enforcement almost immediately, prompted by neighborhood complaints and the club's lack of a dance permit. Katz argued that the club was as a public hall under city code, exempt from the requirement for a dance permit. The club's listed

The pit at a punk show at Crest Theatre, circa 1985. Prior to its restoration as a movie theater in 1986, the Crest was frequently used as a concert venue. *Photo by John Muheim.*

Hot Spit Dancers at last Club Minimal show. Left to right: Vince Voodoo (vocals); Theron (bass); Nick Kappos, aka Big Nick Slurb (guitar); and Ronnie (drums). *Photo by John Muheim.*

The Toy Dolls at Club Minimal on January 12, 1984. Stewart Katz is on the left with baseball cap. *Photo by John Muheim.*

Los Angeles deathrock band 45 Grave, headliner of the last show at Club Minimal. *Photo by John Muheim.*

capacity of ninety-eight people was below the city's minimum threshold of one hundred. Finally, many Sacramento music venues lacked a dance permit but were allowed to operate, raising the question of selective enforcement of the dance permit law.

Nevertheless, police repeatedly closed down shows using permit issues as justification and said complaints about noise and trash were sufficient reason to deny a permit. In late July, Katz was denied a legal injunction blocking the city from harassing the club. He decided the best way to draw attention was an old-fashioned protest march. At 1:00 p.m. on July 29, 1983, more than one hundred local punks joined Katz at the Tunes to Go record store at 1019 K Street and marched to city hall at 915 I Street. Many came dressed in the most outrageous outfits they had, including leather jackets and spiked collars, combat boots and Chuck Taylors, as well as sporting multicolored and spiked hair. Katz traded his usual baseball cap and Hawaiian shirt for a suit and tie. The crowd's appearance drew as much attention as their demonstrations of slam dancing and skateboard tricks on the way to City Hall. City of Sacramento staff was apparently convinced of the group's sincerity, because they issued a dance permit to Club Minimal the following day.[95]

Club Minimal's minimalist aesthetic was moderated by a skate ramp, elevated stage and sound board and art installations by Steve Vanoni and Marco Fuoco, supplemented by visitors' regular tags and spray-bombings on the walls. Touring bands like Black Flag, Toy Dolls, MDC, TSOL and the Circle Jerks were supported by local bands, including the Lamos, the Vacant, Dead Pledge, Forced Tradition, Rebel Truth, Square Cools, Groovie Ghoulies and the Hot Spit Dancers. Some of these bands played harder and faster than 1977 punk, eschewing New Wave influences in favor of pure speed, known as hardcore. Legal status did not end official scrutiny, but shows were stopped by police less often, making them more financially viable.

To report on the scene and inform people of upcoming shows, Katz started *Saczine*, which was distributed at local clubs, record stores and cafés. *Saczine* was soon joined by *SPAMM*, an independent 'zine written by Scott Soriano, in October 1983. *SPAMM* featured interviews with local and touring bands, record reviews and Scott's perspectives on the state of the local scene. The first issue's editorial justified the need for a local publication focused on punk:

> *I figured Sacto has a real cool scene with cool bands, but who knows about it? Besides scene reports in* [MAXIMUMROCKRNROLL] *and other small zines, and the Rebel Truth tour, hardly anyone knows about Sacto. Even punx in Sacto don't know about Sacto (ever hear of the RPMs, the RC Boys, or the Socially Unexcepted?) So this is meant to fill a void that has been unfilled for far too long. We've got a scene, bands, 2 clubs, a radio station that occasionally plays* [hardcore] *(KDVS) & a radio station that plays some '77 punk (KPOP). We needed a fanzine. This is it. So this is what I have to say to all the non Sacto readerz. It's time to wake up 'cos someone's disgracing the capitol!*
> —Scott Soriano, editorial, SPAMM No. 1

The other club was Vortograph, a former railroad express warehouse at Fifteenth and C Streets. Managed by Bartley Cavanaugh III, grandson of former Sacramento city manager Bart Cavanaugh, Vortograph received its dance permit in December 1983. Like Club Minimal, it was an all-ages club for live bands. Vortograph also featured DJ dance nights under the name Club Vortex, managed by promoter Jerry Perry, who got his start at Kin's Coloma. The City of Sacramento forbade for-profit live music and dance events at city park facilities like Clunie Hall in McKinley Park, ending the

Left: Young people at Club Vortograph, located at Fifteenth and C Streets, circa 1985. Boots and spiked belts were prohibited in the club; Johnny (center) is carrying his combat boots. *Photo courtesy of Heidi Bennett.*

Below: Tales of Terror at the final Club Minimal show on June 16, 1984: *Left to right*: Jeff Magner, Pat "Rat's Ass" Stratford, Lyon Wong, Thopper Jaw and Trip Mender. *Photo by John Muheim.*

all-ages Zu Club held at Clunie, so Club Vortex filled another need for local all-ages entertainment.

Club Minimal closed in June 1984, bowing to continued pressure from police and city government despite the dance permit. Katz also grew weary of the additional difficulties of running a club, including repairing damage to the building after shows. Police harassment and a perceived lack of appreciation from those attending the shows meant that running Club Minimal was not much fun and not profitable enough to justify the effort. After shutting the doors of Club Minimal, Katz continued booking shows until about 1989. He also attended law school, driven by his repeated conflicts with police and city officials, and became an attorney focusing on civil rights and police brutality cases. Interviewed in *SPAMM* number five after the closure of the club, he explained why he kept booking punk shows despite so many setbacks and obstacles. Katz remarked, "Whenever I used to get a little, Oh my God, why am I doing this? type pang, I'd check out Danseparc or Lord Beaverbrooks [two mainstream Sacramento nightclubs] and say, Oh yeah, that's why—I hate these places!"[96]

TALES OF TERROR

Club Minimal nurtured many local punk bands, but the most iconic was Tales of Terror. Formed in 1982, lead singer Pat Stratford, nicknamed Rat's Ass, was already a veteran of the Square Cools and the RC Boys, as was bass player Jeff Magner, better known as Boots or Dusty Coffin. Formed after the breakup of the Square Cools, Tales of Terror enlisted drummer Mike Hunter (aka Thopper Jaw) and guitarist Lyon Wong (aka Luther Storms or Emperor Fuckshit). Lyon was the son of actor and Stucco Factory resident artist Victor Wong. The Stucco Factory became a rehearsal space for the newly formed band. The young musicians were part of the Rancho Cordova skating scene, and Tales of Terror played like Rancho Cordova street skaters shredded, with total abandon, instinctive skill and an utter disregard for personal safety.

The band quickly established a local following and became regulars at Club Minimal. In early 1984, it toured the western United States, including Los Angeles and Santa Barbara, California; Las Vegas, Nevada; Phoenix, Arizona; Seattle, Washington; Portland and Eugene, Oregon. The band returned with a second guitarist, Captain Trip Mender (Steve Hunt), but without its manager, who grew so tired of the band's antics that he dropped off the trailer containing the band and their equipment and left the musicians by the side of the road.

We went to Eugene, which was pretty boring, except for this party where we threw furniture off of a balcony, and got them evicted, but they want us to come back.

—Rat's Ass

The summer of 1984 brought more touring and the band's self-titled album, *Tales of Terror*. In between recording and touring, Tales of Terror played the last show at Club Minimal, opening for Los Angeles deathrock legends 45 Grave. Local shows became harder to find, so the band found other places to play, including live shows at the Stucco Factory. Steve Vanoni documented a Tales of Terror show at Stucco Factory for use in a film project, capturing the band's frantic energy and a cross-section of the Sacramento creative scene, crowded into the art-laden metal warehouse. Despite the poor acoustics of the room and the high alcohol content of the musicians, the band's style superseded the simplified high-speed approach of hardcore but avoided overly complex solos. Lyrics were crude, sarcastic, nihilistic and frequently obscene. The band's approach precluded taking its music too seriously. The album saw only limited production with about 5,000 copies, but some of those copies ended up in the hands of musicians in the Pacific Northwest, becoming a major influence on grunge bands Mudhoney, Nirvana and Pearl Jam. Mudhoney's Mark Arm covered a Tales of Terror song with his earlier band Green River and considered their live show among the greatest he had ever seen. Kurt Cobain's notebooks indicated the troubled musician considered their album among his favorites. Interviews with the band indicate that they had big dreams, not taken too seriously. "Go as far as possible. Be rock gods, have fun, abuse our livers. We're turning our stage show into more of a sideshow. We don't really care if we're in tune, as long as we have fun. We're getting into the three-ring circus chaos effect. That goes along with our new cult, the Evil Empire. It's a group of people that we think are obnoxious enough," said lead singer Rat's Ass.

On January 5, 1986, Lyon Wong was verbally accosted by a group of teenagers in a pickup truck near the Zebra Club on Nineteenth and P Streets. Lyon shouted back, and the teenagers pulled over and attacked. Lyon was struck to the ground and his head hit the curb, causing fatal trauma. The student who struck Lyon received only six months in jail for Lyon's death. Afterward, the surviving bandmates decided not to continue as Tales of Terror. All formed other bands, but none with Tales of Terror's bombastic chemistry.[97]

PUNK VENUES OF THE 1980S

China Wagon, a Chinese restaurant on Broadway and Nineteenth Street, first opened as Sam's Ranch Wagon. In 1980, it became a New Wave music venue, booked by promoter Carol Gale and her boyfriend, Bo Richards, former manager of Ozzie, under the name Can't Tell Productions. Gale and Richards focused on New Wave, but sometimes included bands from San Francisco's second wave of punk, like Flipper and the Dead Kennedys, supported by local acts. "Bands are popping up all over and this gives them a chance to play, and it gives other people a chance to hear them. Locally it's a chance to encourage the scene," said Gale in an interview with *Suttertown News*. The China Wagon's live music era ended in 1981, when it briefly became Molly's Place, a male burlesque club, but Molly's was also short-lived, cut short by an April 1979 ordinance that forbade new adult cabaret establishments without a special permit.[98]

Like Stewart Katz with Club Minimal, Gale and Richards sought their own venue, along with business partner Sandra Lim. They were able to leverage a $30,000 loan from the Sacramento Housing and Redevelopment Agency and $125,000 in private investment to refurbish the Esquire Theater at Thirteenth and K Streets. Their plans included a café and espresso bar, beer, wine and food, in addition to rock concerts, a dance club and movies. Originally planning on an April 1984 opening, construction delays meant the grand opening was not held until late September. The club was welcomed by those interested in revitalizing K Street, and investment by SHRA gave Club Can't Tell limited protection from city harassment. Underneath Club Can't Tell was the Metro Bar & Grill, previously known by several names, including the Hickory House, Upstairs/Downstairs and the Underground Shingle. The venue also hosted comedy and dance nights and had a long-standing gay clientele.

Live shows at Club Can't Tell were a mixture of mainstream, avant-garde and college rock acts, from Tower of Power to the Red Hot Chili Peppers. Stewart Katz occasionally rented Club Can't Tell for touring punk and metal bands, while local acts Macabre Shocks and Vicious Gel were featured at local band nights. Marco Fuoco's Screaming Pygmy Orchestra performance

Heavy metal fans wait outside the Crest Theatre before a concert featuring Slayer and Venom. *Photo by John Muheim.*

Jello Biafra of the Dead Kennedys performing at the Crest Theatre on April 29, 1983. *Photo by John Muheim.*

at Club Can't Tell featured "seven poets, five Mexican musicians, three female Modern dancers, two comics from the group RSVP, an actor, four saxophonists, 10 percussionists, guitarist Robert Kuhlman of Flying Boats…bassist Charles DeWitt and an electric ukulele player."[99]

Despite an optimistic beginning, 1985 proved a rough year for Sacramento's punk scene. In April, the Vortograph lost its dance permit. City officials cited complaints about vandalism, noise and drinking near the club. In 1986, Sacramento skater turned recording engineer John Baccigaluppi opened Enharmonik Studios in the upper story of Vortograph's building at Fifteenth and C Streets. Also in April, Club Can't Tell filed Chapter 11 due to financial trouble after Sandra Lim left the partnership. Improvements like the planned café and restaurant were never completed. In October, the city of Sacramento modified its dance permit ordinance, reducing the minimum capacity requiring a permit to fifty people.

The Oasis Ballroom at Twentieth and I Streets, home of rock-and-roll shows since its days as Crabshaw Corner in 1972, came under fire in 1982 when neighbors grew increasingly concerned about noise and vandalism centered around the club. Over time, the club hosted a diverse array of performers including Jerry Garcia and Van Morrison, Elvin Bishop and John Lee Hooker. By the 1980s they also hosted touring acts like the Toy Dolls and Camper Van Beethoven, supported by local punk bands like the Sea Hags. The club was limited to those older than 16, providing a venue for some of the local teenage audience.

City council member David Shore, who lived a block away, considered the club's location in a residential neighborhood inappropriate. In June 1986, neighbors attempted to revoke the Oasis's dance permit, testifying to Mac Mailes, the same city administrator who resisted granting a permit to Club Minimal in 1983 and revoked the Vortograph's permit in 1985. Stewart Katz, who occasionally promoted punk shows at the Oasis, testified in the club's defense, along with musician/journalist Jackson Griffith. Club owner Dave Dittman testified that other nearby bars, a twenty-four-hour convenience store, a liquor store and the nearby prostitutes' stroll on Seventeenth Street were hazards to neighborhood safety more serious than the Oasis, and Sacramento police concurred with Dittman's assessment. Neighbors accused the police department of failing to follow up on neighborhood complaints about the venue and claimed police were underreporting calls because the Oasis hired off-duty police as security staff. Mailes refused to revoke the permit, claiming that the Oasis's owners were making a good faith effort to address neighborhood problems. Despite this victory, Dittman closed the club in July 1986, citing the draining effect of long-term struggles with the neighbors and a dwindling audience for live music.[100]

Club Can't Tell continued hosting shows until November 1987. Its final live show featured music and poetry by Jim Carroll and Steve Vanoni.[101] Despite their city funding, completion of the Hyatt Regency across K Street brought pressure by the hotel to rid K Street of young people who might intimidate tourists. Just as the Hyatt's construction brought destruction to the Francesca Apartments, it ended Richards and Gale's experiment on K Street. Downstairs dance club and bar Metro Metro continued operation until the mid-1990s. Hardcore band 7 Seconds recorded a live set performed at Club Can't Tell, combined with tracks recorded at Sacramento's El Dorado Saloon, mixed at Enharmonik Studio and released as "Live! One Plus One" in 1987.

POSITIVE HARDCORE WITH KEVIN SECONDS

The band 7 Seconds formed in Reno, Nevada, in 1980, but two of its founding members, Kevin and Steve Marvelli (better known as Kevin Seconds and Steve Youth), were born in Sacramento. Their family moved to Reno in 1976, and the brothers discovered punk the following year. Because Sacramento was the closest large city to Reno and on the way to the Bay Area, it was a natural touring stop for 7 Seconds, which played at early venues like Kin's Coloma, Club Minimal and Club Can't Tell. Visits to Sacramento were inspiring to Kevin, who hoped to spur similar all-ages punk venues in Reno but met even more obstacles from the local authorities, who were more interested in the strictly adults-only entertainment offered by Reno's casino industry.

> *At that time, we were so excited that the kids created their own scene in cities of similar size to Sacramento and Reno...I think our first legit show was at Galactica 2000, in 1981 with UK Decay and Social Unrest...I was too young to remember what Midtown was like, we were from the 'burbs and would go "Ooh, big city, big buildings!" But then, [in] 81–82, we'd come down here, and it felt like a big, crazy city—"No one's on the street, it must be really dangerous to be here!" The Rebel Truth guys became really good friends. We would just trade shows, and I always got the feeling that Sacramento always had really cool 'zines and there was just a really great underground scene that started brewing really quickly.*

To me, Sacramento was cooler than San Francisco—cool shows, cool underground things going on—but less artsy-fartsy, kids like us were doing things. [San Francisco] was cool, too; I liked that, but I never felt totally—I felt like it wasn't inclusive, I didn't feel like I could be a part of that at all. I was searching, I always wanted something that was not like all my friends—listening to Deep Purple and Black Sabbath, cruising Downtown was the thing to do, trying to get chicks. But it was never my thing, and I never felt completely comfortable.

I wasn't a party kid. I tried, but I was just, "There's got to be more to life than being sixteen and doing this bullshit." And I didn't know what it was, because I knew I wanted to be in a band. But when I was growing up, to see a band you had to go to an arena with twenty thousand people; you couldn't just go to clubs. There were no all-ages shows. You couldn't go to a club, and even if you [did,] they were all bands doing…Molly Hatchet covers or whatever. And disco was the big thing, being this young teenage kid with these ideas was really frustrating. And growing up in Reno was doubly frustrating because nothing was about kids. It was all about twenty-one and over, gambling, drinking, prostitution. It had nothing to do with anybody underage, so I think it was the perfect catalyst for us to start our own scene in Reno. Later on, we realized that this was happening all over the country! Kids in Dayton, Ohio, were doing that; kids in the middle of Texas were doing that. It was good to know that it was happening, [that] we're not the only misfits who are just sitting here thinking you're suffering.

Perhaps due to Reno's emphasis on alcohol and adults, Kevin and his bandmates became part of the Straight Edge movement. Straight Edge bands took a different direction from the apparently nihilistic and negative tone of punk, including its association with drug abuse and alcoholic excess. Washington, D.C. hardcore band Minor Threat's song "Straight Edge" became an anthem eschewing alcohol, drugs, cigarettes and even sex. This positive spin on punk did not mean a reduction in speed, intensity or volume. Some assumed (incorrectly) that 7 Seconds's name was taken from the average length of its songs, which were short and fast, vocals shouted rather than sung and larded with obscenities that shocked local Reno music journalists. Over time many Straight Edge bands mellowed in breakneck playing speed and their hardline stance about abstinence but persevered as musicians, avoiding the "live fast, die young" ethos that brought many bright young musicians to tragic ends. Touring brought Kevin back to his hometown, where he liked what he saw.

7 Seconds at Club Can't Tell performing "99 Red Balloons." Club Can't Tell was located inside the Esquire Theater at Fourteenth and K Streets. *Photo by John Muheim.*

7 Seconds in the wreckage of the Clunie Hotel at Eighth and K Streets, circa 1988. *Left to right*: Kevin Seconds (vocals), Steve Youth (bass), Troy Mowat (drums) and Bobby Adams (guitar). *Photo by John Muheim.*

It was magical, because Stewart lived over on N, just up the street. We'd come to play a show in Sacramento, usually at Club Can't Tell. We'd stop at Stewart's place to take a shower, and then he'd walk us over to Java City and get an espresso. It felt like we were in a totally crazy, vibrant little scene right on the street, and I thought, "I want that, I want to be a part of that!" It really wasn't that big a deal, but it was something we tried to get started in Reno but just couldn't—a community of people hanging out, playing chess, starting bands, doing music, it was a pretty cool thing. And I met my future wife at that Java City, so…back then it was scary after Java City closed; walking up the street, I'd always have a screwdriver because once a guy attacked me with a screwdriver walking down that street, and I figured I'd carry a screwdriver of my own—that was my weapon of choice!

In 1988, Stewart Katz became 7 Seconds's manager, and he invited them to live in Sacramento. Kevin was happy to be closer to his hometown, but his bandmates found conditions less than ideal. They returned to Reno, but Kevin decided to stay. He remained a member of 7 Seconds but began performing solo in Sacramento, booking shows at coffee shops.

The band had moved into his office building, we literally slept on boxes of T-shirts. We had a sink but not a shower, so we had friends who would pick us up [so we could] *take a shower at their house*[s]. *It was grim; it was really bad. But I just knew that I wanted to be back in Sac at the time. I loved Midtown and rent was cheap, and I needed to get out of Reno. I got the band to all come down. We had an apartment on Twenty-fifth and H. We all had this one-bedroom apartment that was just trashed…The four of us were living there; we had no furniture—we had a microwave. The rest of the guys really didn't want to live in Sacramento. I loved the town and met a couple friends. Sacramento was so good to 7 Seconds, we had great shows, Stewart was really supportive and said he would find us an apartment. He found us an apartment, but* [my band mates] *just hated it, packed up and left. I lived in New York with my girlfriend for a while… on and off in New York for about three years. I'd live here, go on tour and live in New York for a couple of months. I was sort of pretending I was on two coasts. It was great because I never got sick of New York and never got sick of Sacramento.*

PUNK HOUSES AND THE NEXT STEPS OF THE DIY MOVEMENT

Some shows happened at even less formal spaces, called punk houses. Typically located in rental houses owned by absentee landlords, unconcerned about loud tenants as long as rent was paid, a punk house was primarily a residence, with rent split as many ways as possible, but it also became practice space for the next wave of Sacramento punk bands. One of Sacramento's earliest punk houses of note was Bert House at 1901 I Street, from around 1985 to 1990. Bert House was home to local bands, including Sewer Trout, Pollution Circus, Sins of the Flesh and the New Vulgarians. This new generation of bands, often connected with the Gilman Street project and Lookout Records in Berkeley (Lookout released records by Sacramento bands such as Sewer Trout and the Groovie Ghoulies), took the DIY ethic another step beyond Club Minimal by organizing volunteer-run, nonprofit shows with an anticapitalist philosophy.[102]

Punks on the porch of Reverend Randy's house at Twenty-second and F Streets. Penny Crane and Leon Phaby are in the foreground. *Photo courtesy of Heidi Miller.*

The name BERT stood for "Bert and Ernie Rock Together" and was home to scene stalwarts like Hot Spit Dancers guitarist Big Nick Slurb, activists Emily Murdock and Craig Usher and sidewalk artist Ground Chuck. Punk houses also served as impromptu social spaces, and many practice sessions turned into de facto live shows when friends with beer showed up to watch or when punk house residents decided a house party needed musical accompaniment. They also served as free hostels for touring bands and visiting punks traveling the country. According to Dennis Yudt, "If you had a funny haircut in those days, you probably passed out on a couch there [at] one time or another."[103] Despite its crises and brushes with violence, challenges from authority and official indifference, Sacramento's punk scene grew. New live music venues—including the Cattle Club on the far end of East Sacramento; the Guild Theatre in Oak Park; and Old Ironsides, which began hosting live music in 1991—opened. Other venues appeared in cafés, which became Midtown's most prominent bohemian community spaces.

7

Living in Java City

Pava's…What makes a place worth waiting for, for half an hour or forty minutes, to have dinner or breakfast? It's pretty elusive. It's got to be somehow the environment—it's a nice place or it's a scene…Why would people go there? You ran into friends; that's where everybody was going. It had become a social center, a social event. Your friends and peers were there, so you run into them, say hi, have breakfast with them. Your peers were at the table next to you or across from you. And it was a nice breakfast!
—David Houston

In his book *The Great Good Place*, sociologist Ray Oldenburg identified "third places" as locations separate from home and workplace (first and second places), where people congregate to meet each other in planned or unplanned fashion. They are informal gathering places and social spaces, including restaurants, bars and coffee shops, art galleries, parks and festivals and retail shops like record stores and bookstores. Oldenburg felt that America's suburbanization created a national deficit of third places, losing historic institutions like neighborhood bars, social clubs and teen centers. Public spaces became structured, privatized environments, with the shopping mall as the ultimate example of controlled, segregated, privately owned public space. The hurried pace of consumer culture meant an institutional environment where quick turnover of tables discouraged long chats over coffee. The drive-through restaurant meant customers never entered the restaurant or left their car, eliminating casual social interaction with other customers.[104]

Sam's Hof Brau, located in the Kost Building at Eighteenth and J Streets, was an important venue for Sacramento blues bands, even if local music ordinances prohibited dancing. *Photo by Joe Perfecto.*

Midtown never entirely lost its third places, and new places appeared to meet their needs of the influx of new urban migrants. In Midtown, café owners like Lee Page and Masako Yniguez challenged the city's limitations on sidewalk dining. Diners on the sidewalk, under umbrella tables or Midtown's generous tree canopy, became an attraction for pedestrians strolling by, presenting a lively human atmosphere instead of a clear sidewalk devoid of human activity. At the same time, diners on the sidewalk were equally entertained by the dance of people on the street walking past, a social transaction that benefited both groups. Even those in cars driving through the neighborhood shared this benefit, as pedestrian activity signaled safety to those unfamiliar with the neighborhood. Because most of these Midtown gathering places had no parking lots, these visitors usually had to park somewhere else in the neighborhood, joining the social dance of the street.

For their customers, these retail locations were social spaces, but they were also places of employment. The nature of the business allowed a greater level of personal freedom of expression in appearance and dress, thanks to the more tolerant nature of the neighborhood. In the 1980s, outrageous hairstyles and color, piercings and tattoos were far less socially acceptable

Alex Rask, manager of Falor's Coffee Bar, and Falor's massive Hobart coffee grinder, inside the Public Market at 13th and J Street, 1975. *Center for Sacramento History, Sacramento Bee collection.*

than in the twenty-first century, especially in a suburban environment, but they were tolerated in Midtown.

I went about getting a job right away, which was at "Bagful of Bagels." I was working there and quickly became the assistant manager, a seventeen-year-old assistant manager with really high hair and…I got to look like a weirdo and give really great customer service!…For a while it was a total weirdo fest. [Owner] *Rob Boriskin was really open minded when it came to hiring creative, weird-looking people as long as we knew how to do our jobs.*

—Heidi Miller

MIDTOWN'S EARLY COFFEEHOUSES

Sacramento's tradition of gourmet coffee shops probably began at Falor's Coffee Bar. In 1928, Falor's opened in Sacramento's Public Market building, the Julia Morgan–designed retail complex at Thirteenth and J Streets. The café was founded by Richard Falor, a World War I veteran, who started with a massive Hobart coffee grinder and three stools. He roasted the coffee daily on site in small batches, using premium beans. To demonstrate its superior flavor, he served samples to potential customers. When customers started asking for doughnuts or cookies with their coffee, Falor added a restaurant. Rhubarb pie and chicken and biscuits, made fresh every day, were the house specialties. Using high-quality Guatemalan beans, Falor's was expensive but unmatched in quality. The restaurant served over one thousand customers per day but intentionally ran out of food each day at about 1:30 in the afternoon to ensure it would start with fresh items each morning.

In May 1975, Falor's closed its doors. Manager Alex Rask blamed slow business on Convention Center construction and less appreciation of high-quality baked goods and coffee that could not compete with frozen food and canned coffee at cheaper restaurants. Rask noted that young hippies were an exception: "They seem to know good food when they eat it…we've never resorted to using substitutes or lowered our standards."[105]

The hippies acquired a taste for quality coffee, but cafés were more than just places to eat. In Oak Park, artist Sal Yniguez opened the Belmonte Coffee Shop at 2975 Thirty-fifth Street in 1962, a beatnik café inhabited by artists like Wayne Thiebaud, Gregory Kondos and Russ Solomon. Hipsters and beatniks from CSUS and Sacramento State, artists and musicians all found refuge at the Belmonte. Yniguez connected the café experience with art, music and an atmosphere that promoted culture, creating a "third space" for countercultural life, but he closed the Belmonte as Oak Park became more dangerous during the social upheavals of the late 1960s.

Midtown's first coffee shop of note was Giovanni's on Twentieth and I Streets, founded by John DeGeiso in 1973. In 1975, DeGeiso sold the business to Home Front founder Lee Page. Giovanni's offered twenty-nine varieties of coffee from around the world, including Ethiopian and Jamaican beans, with prices ranging from thirty-five cents for a large cup of house blend to ninety-five cents for a Café Borgia, a mixture of espresso, whipped cream, chocolate and spices.[106] Page later relocated around the corner on Twenty-first Street, renaming the shop the Weatherstone in 1977, taking over a space previously occupied by the Down Home Gallery, a 1960s art gallery. Weatherstone featured big couches, a piano and an enormous unabridged dictionary on a stand. Proximity to a laundromat and the nearby Oasis Ballroom drew a mixed crowd of nearby residents and music fans. Pastries and coffee were delivered regularly from San Francisco. According to Gerald Thomas, Weatherstone in the 1970s was the preferred café for marijuana smokers, and customers often toked openly at the café's sidewalk tables. Because city codes prohibited restaurants from serving on sidewalks, the outside tables drew more official attention than the pot smoke. Traffic on Twenty-first Street in the 1970s was so light that a popular pastime among Weatherstone regulars was to place bets on how long a Twinkie placed in the road would survive unmolested before being squashed by a passing car. Weatherstone closed in 1987 but reopened in 1988 under new ownership, the first expansion of Sacramento roaster Java City.[107]

Now, I realized across the street there was this old coffeehouse [Weatherstone], *which we'd kid about getting high as you walked by, because…all the people came to smoke pot there! And Lee, the owner, was a wonderful guy, and his wife. They opened at eight in the morning and closed at eight at night, and there was a laundromat* [next door].
—Dale Kooyman

Located at 2330 K Street, Pava's immediately became a neighborhood institution upon its opening in 1974. Focusing on fresh ingredients and whole grains, Pava's was not strictly a health food restaurant but emphasized fresh and healthy alternatives, including vegetarian entrees. Furnished with

Pava's at Twenty-fourth and K Streets was a favorite brunch destination in Midtown from 1974 until it was destroyed by fire in 1990. *Photo by Joe Perfecto.*

antiques and flowers, the restaurant drew a fanatically loyal clientele from the neighborhood and beyond. The eggs Benedict and daily crêpe specials were as well known as the long lines for a table at weekend brunches. Pava's, like others among its generation of Midtown cafes and restaurants, encouraged customers to linger, communicate and break bread together. The restaurant caught fire on June 29, 1990, destroying the building.[108]

From '73–'75, people started to buy up properties on K Street and start enclaves of businesses. Pava's was the meeting place for almost everybody, politicians like Lloyd Connelly, Phil Isenberg, and that's when the businesses started coming back…up to that point we had coffee shops, that was one of the first real breakfast places where you could have a leisurely breakfast, eggs Benedict, more in the sophisticated line. If they were around today they would be the first to do sustainable organic, a "third place," really trying to build community.

—Maryellen Burns

EYE DREAM AND LUNA'S CAFÉ

Teens in the bathroom of Eye Dream Ice Cream in June 1984 shortly before the building was demolished. *Center for Sacramento History,* Suttertown News *collection.*

Located on Twenty-first Street between K and L Streets, Eye Dream was one of the earliest Midtown coffee houses to stay open until midnight, opening in 1982 in an ice cream shop previously named Yum's. It featured Bud's ice cream, vegetarian snacks and high-quality coffee. Owner Gary Lehar displayed the work of local artists. Local poets and bands performed in the evenings. Located just three blocks south of Weatherstone, Eye Dream catered to a younger crowd. Regulars included Steve Vanoni, Victor Wong and other members of the Stucco Factory scene.

Next door to Eye Dream were two nightclubs, Club 21 and the Rose. In April 1984, the Cal-Western Life Insurance Company, which owned the lot where all three businesses sat, ordered them to close. Cal-Western's main office was located across the street, and it claimed a greater need for employee parking. Gary Lehar attempted to prevent his café's closure, calling on councilmember David Shore and state assembly member Lloyd Connelly to assist. Despite "gracious arm-twisting" by Connelly, a self-described regular at Eye Dream, and a study by a city traffic engineer that showed Cal-Western could fit at least twenty-five more cars into its existing lots if they were more efficiently arranged, Cal-Western proceeded with the eviction and demolition. Some felt that the reason behind the demolition was official discomfort with the presence of a gay bar, black nightclub and punk coffee shop across from the company's headquarters, but others considered it purely a fiscal consideration. Despite the efforts of Shore and Connelly, the insurance company did not relent. Eye Dream held a final event in June 1984, and the site was cleared shortly thereafter.[109]

Left: Punks at Eye Dream Café, Twenty-first and L Streets, salute the camera shortly before the building was demolished for a parking lot. *Center for Sacramento History*, Suttertown News *collection.*

Below: Art Luna and his sister Chris opened Luna's Café in 1983 at 1414 Sixteenth Street, previously the Grinding Stone coffeehouse. *Center for Sacramento History*, Suttertown News *collection.*

Just before I moved down here I used to go to Eye Dream because I had a girlfriend who lived around the corner…It was an ice cream place. This was before Java City; it was sort of like the Weatherstone. It was one of the few places you could sit outside and get something to eat or drink. I moved down here the same year that Java City opened, and I think that was one of the first places you could sit outside and hang out. There just weren't places—I remember Weatherstone, Java City and Eye Dream as being the only places down here that did that.

—Mark Miller

Art Luna and his sister Chris opened a juice stand on Eighth and K Streets, circa 1980, using the profits from selling *licuados* to open a short-lived restaurant in the Bay Area. Returning to Sacramento in 1983, they leased the former Grinding Stone café, operated by local blues musician Nate Shiner, at 1414 Sixteenth Street. Luna's Café featured quality coffee, fresh fruit and vegetable juices, sandwiches and quesadillas and scrambled eggs cooked with espresso machine steam. The walls showcased the work of local Chicana artists, including that of *Las Co-Madres Artistas* members. Their small stage hosted jazz bands, stand-up comedy and poetry, including RCAF founder José Montoya's weekly poetry series. Unlike the short-lived Eye Dream, Luna's has persevered for more than thirty years.[110]

JAVA CITY

After the loss of Eye Dream, Java City became the iconic Midtown coffee shop of the 1980s. Founded by former state employee Tom Weborg and coffee roaster Steve Priley at Eighteenth and Capitol in 1985, Java City's roasting operation filled the neighborhood with a distinct aroma that drew residents from Midtown and workers from Downtown office buildings. While Coffeeworks, located at Thirty-fourth Street and Folsom Boulevard, started roasting on site in 1982, it was too remote to attract the combination of state employees and the new generation of Midtown coffee enthusiasts who lived near the recently closed Eye Dream coffeehouse. In 1986, Java City hosted its first poetry marathon, the 127-hour brainchild of local poet Bari Kennedy, who first held poetry marathons in 1983 and 1984 at Café Croissant on Ninth and K Streets. The poetry marathons and high-quality coffee cemented Java City as Midtown's cultural epicenter. At night, Java City was the only open business for blocks, an oasis of light at Eighteenth and Capitol. The neighborhood was far less safe than it is today. Young women on their way to Java City were sometimes propositioned by passing cars, mistaken for the streetwalkers who worked near Georgian's Casino on J Street or the Seventeenth Street stroll. Java City became a cross-section of the city. New Wave shop girls in leopard print coats and cat-eye glasses, poets, musicians and artists trading work and opinions, punks and skinheads in flight jackets and Doc Martens, recovering alcoholics and addicts taking a break from AA meetings at nearby Group One, bikers, retirees, office workers, urban professionals and disabled residents of nearby board-and-care homes all became part of the urban fabric at Java City.

Weborg originally envisioned Java City as a wholesaler, but the storefront generated so much walk-up business that seats and tables were added inside and outside the shop. Outside seating was facilitated by an enormous camphor tree planted in 1886 that shaded the sidewalk, providing respite from summer heat and a comfortable atmosphere. Former employee Nick Roberts, who worked at Java City in 1991–92, said that the job could be frustrating, due to the sometimes too-close eye of supervisors (who sometimes took disciplinary action for "looking depressed at work"), but he, like many employees, spent almost as much time hanging out at Java City as he did working. "Even after I got off work, I'd still find myself there—virtually everyone I knew would be there." In addition to the social scene, the drinks were excellent. Roberts waxed poetic about the "Fro-Mo," a chocolatey mixture of gelato and espresso. "Whenever anyone ordered it, I deliberately made too much, and saved the extra for myself!"

Midtown, back then rents [were] *still cheap. Midtown was just where all the beatniks, freaks, punks* [were]; [it was] *where you'd find gay people. All the people who were ostracized, Midtown welcomed them. Going to poetry readings* [at] *Webber's Books, it was really what I needed and what I craved, without having to go to San Francisco or New York. In Reno, we didn't have that, and* [in] *Sacramento* [it] *just seemed, like, I'm finally back where I was born… The good stuff outweighed, the people I met even when we first started coming in* [the] *'80s, when it was a more "new wavey" scene as opposed to hardcore, we met some great people. I think I was always thinking about coming back, it just seemed so much more happening than Reno, at least back then! To me, it was everything that we wanted to see when I'd go to Java City and hang out with all my buddies on the corner. It was where you'd go to find out what was happening that night.*
—Kevin Seconds

The yuppification of Midtown was apparent by 1982, when the former space occupied by Jodette's free store and Juliana's Kitchen organic restaurant became Fiasco, a wine bar that advertised over fifty Chardonnays. *Center for Sacramento History,* Suttertown News *collection.*

In 1988, Drago's Café opened at 2326 K Street, next door to Pava's. Drago's was the product of Dragan Lazetich, son of Pava Lazetich, the original owner of Pava's. Drago's featured a large outdoor patio, an extension of the building's front porch, and like Java City, it deliberately fostered a European coffeehouse atmosphere. It became the host of cultural events, including poetry readings and improvisational theater, such as Victor Wong's "K-RAP Radio Players" show. Unlike Java City, where only coffee and nonalcoholic beverages were served, Drago's also carried beer and wine. The café changed owners in 1991, reopening as Café Montreal with a greater emphasis on live music. West of Drago's, Rick's Dessert Diner moved into the former Failasouf Shop in 1986.

Not every café was in Midtown, but they were often nearby. Joan Riordan, who moved from Long Beach to attend UC Davis, worked at Café Roma in Davis before opening her own shop, Espresso Metro, in 1988. Located on Eleventh Avenue and Freeport Boulevard in Land Park, the building was once the first location of Sacramento State University before the permanent location in East Sacramento was built. Her location just north of Sacramento City College reflected her experience running a college-adjacent café in Davis.

Espresso Metro founder Joan Riordan and the "Metromobile," a 1961 Ford Falcon delivery
sedan, outside Espresso Metro on Eleventh Avenue, circa 1991. *Photo by Jennifer Hogan,
courtesy of Joan Riordan.*

The shop quickly became a favorite of students; local politicians, including Joe
Serna and Phil Isenberg; and musicians like Ray Rill. In 1992, Joan expanded
to a second location at Eleventh and K Streets, on the heart of the K Street
mall, operated by her sister-in-law, Patricia Castleberry.[111]

In 1989, a long-abandoned 1893 firehouse on Nineteenth and L Streets,
used by heroin addicts as a shooting gallery, became a coffeehouse called
New Helvetia. In 1990, Allyson Dalton, daughter of the owners of Fox &
Goose, opened Greta's Café at Nineteenth and Capitol, in between Java
City and New Helvetia, focusing on fresh baked goods produced in-house.
No Jive Java, an upstart operation run by former Java City employees,
opened up right next door to Java City in 1992, offering lower prices
and later hours, but it only lasted a few years. Capitol Garage opened at
Fifteenth and L Streets in 1992 as a late-night café. Its corner parking lot
hosted live music and poetry, including artists like Michael Psycho, Jackson
Griffith, Anton Barbeau, Audrey St. Violet and the Anti-Pop Entourage,
booked by Kevin Seconds.[112]

Retiree Ernest Armstrong regularly strolled along K Street wearing outrageous hats and buttons, making friends despite his hearing loss by carrying a notepad so he could converse in writing. *Photo by Joe Perfecto.*

Java City's reopening of Weatherstone in 1988 was the first of many new locations, including a 1989 shop in the Sutter Galleria, a shopping complex located on J Street underneath the Business Route 80 freeway. By 1990, coffee had become a big business, and Java City expanded into a regional chain, opening shops throughout northern California. Java City's expansion was followed by contraction, as national chains opened franchises on every block, and Java City's regional coffee empire retreated back to Midtown. The flagship location remained at Eighteenth and Capitol, shaded by its camphor tree, until 2012. In that year, Java City ended its retail operation and closed its original location, and the camphor tree was cut down after being diagnosed with verticillium wilt by city arborists.[113]

RECORD STORES, BOOK STORES AND THE TOWER EMPIRE

There was a point where you listen to the music you were listening to in junior high, and then someone gives you a tape that just totally blows your mind. Everything changes. And suddenly those old records are gone, and you're in search of this new stuff.
—Mark Miller

Record stores and bookstores were third spaces at which record and book enthusiasts pursued their own interests and made social connections. Some who started out as young record collectors opened their own shops, like Donnie Jupiter, who went into business with Keith McKee to open Markee Records on K Street in 1977–78. Specializing in collectibles, imports, local records and live bootleg recordings, independent record stores were also informal meeting places, although shop owners sometimes discouraged those more interested in socializing than buying records. Record stores also served a marketing function, providing wall and counter space for local shows via posters, handbills and 'zines.

Records on K Street, opening in 1973, became a record collectors' gold mine. Starting at Ninth and K Street, it relocated to a former clothing store at 710 K Street around 1990, including a cavernous and purportedly haunted basement. The store's sign was designed by underground comic artist Robert Crumb, and a photo of the store's interior became the cover of Sacramento native DJ Shadow's influential album *Endtroducing.* Robert Fauble, who got his start promoting punk shows in Sacramento's suburbs, opened the Beat on H Street in East Sacramento before relocating to Thirty-third and Folsom Boulevard, near Coffeeworks, and moving again to Midtown at Seventeenth and J Streets in 1993. Esoteric Records, founded in 1974, relocated from Alhambra Boulevard to Seventeenth and Broadway in 1982 and then Fifteenth and L Streets in 1994.

Ed Hartmann, owner of Records, 916 K Street, specialized in used and collector records. *Center for Sacramento History,* Suttertown News *collection.*

Esoteric Records became the neighbor of a relocated Beers Books, displaced from its J Street location around the corner from Capitol Garage at Fifteenth and L in 1992 by the Convention Center expansion that doomed the Merrium Apartments. Along with comic book shop Beyond the Pale, located around the corner on Fifteenth Street, the businesses created a synergy of counterculture destinations. Originally opened on J Street by a Mrs. Beers in her husband's electrical shop, Beers Books was sold to Francis Azevedo in 1936, who moved the store twice, arriving at 1406 J Street in 1951, in a former iron foundry. Azevedo sold Beers to Harvey Shank, an Aerojet employee laid off in 1967. In turn, Shank's manager, Bill Senecal, took over operation in 1985. When Levinson's Books closed in 1994 after seventy years, Beers became Sacramento's oldest-surviving bookstore.

Midtown was home to many specialty bookstores, including La Raza Bookstore, women's interest bookstore Lioness Books located at 2224 J Street, collector-oriented Webber's Book Shop at Twenty-first and P, used book specialists River City Books at 912 Twenty-first, Time Tested Books at 1114 Twenty-first and Midtown Books at 1014 Twenty-fourth. May Day Books specialized in leftist/socialist literature from La Semilla Cultural Center at Twentieth and C. Another left-of-center bookstore, New Society Books, stood at 1917A Sixteenth Street. Comic book shop Comics & Comix on the K Street Mall also featured science fiction and fantasy paperbacks.

Above: Harvey Shank (foreground) and Bill Senecal at Beers Books, the oldest surviving bookstore in Sacramento, taken at the store's J Street location. *Center for Sacramento History,* Suttertown News *collection.*

Left: Phil Hoover, manager of Comics & Comix, 921 K Street. Comics & Comix was a regional comic shop company that was founded in Berkeley in 1972 and had two Sacramento stores. *Center for Sacramento History,* Suttertown News *collection.*

The magazine section at Tower Books's Watt Avenue location. Based in Sacramento, Tower had an enormous effect on Sacramento's cultural scene due to its hiring practices and breadth of its inventory. *Center for Sacramento History,* Suttertown News *collection.*

World's Best Comics opened at Thirteenth and J Street as a collaboration between Markee Records' Donnie Jupiter and his bandmate Dave Downey in 1985. World's Best relocated to 1815 K Street in 1988. It closed in 1991 but reopened the same year as House of Monkey thanks to Webber's Books co-owner Doug Webber.[114]

The dominant force in Sacramento's book and record stores was Tower Records, founded in Sacramento by Russ Solomon in 1960 and based out of an office and distribution center in West Sacramento. The first Tower Books, Posters and Plants, opened at 1600 Broadway in 1976. Tower grew into a worldwide retail empire by the 1980s, with enormous breadth of inventory. Like other music and bookstores, Tower became an occupation of choice for local bohemians, both due to its tolerance for unusual fashions and the opportunities it offered for young artists.

Tower stores hired in-store artists who created displays and graphics, and music store employees were often also musicians. Tower's distribution hub in West Sacramento also meant opportunity for Sacramento independent artists and writers via Tower "magazine dude" Doug Biggert. Biggert started out stocking shelves at Tower in 1978, later taking charge of periodical selection for the entire chain. Given a free hand by manager Heidi Keller, whose rule was "Do whatever you want, [but] don't embarrass me," Doug gave locally produced 'zines national exposure by selecting them for worldwide distribution, including both Sacramento-based 'zines and other independently produced publications from around the world. Tower became a common entry in the résumés of many Midtown residents, valued as a creative place to work.

THE CENTER HOLDS

In *The Death and Life of Great American Cities*, Jane Jacobs identified four conditions necessary to generate exuberant diversity on a city's streets. The district must serve more than one function, preferably more than two, to ensure the presence of people on different schedules. Blocks must be short, so people can turn corners often. Buildings must vary in age and condition, including lots of old buildings, with multiple uses on each block. Finally, people must be present, including visitors and workers, but primarily people who live there. By the 1990s, Midtown met each of these conditions as the West End had before redevelopment. Offices and retail stores, sidewalk cafés and restaurants, nightclubs and bars appeared throughout a district with thousands of nearby residents, on a regular street grid with frequent corners and alleys. Old brick warehouses and nineteenth-century Victorians shared those blocks with the ubiquitous dingbat apartments and Modernist office buildings, providing homes, workplaces and creative spaces for more than thirty thousand people. This combination drew thousands of visitors and explorers from throughout the region, inspiring subsequent generations to make their own mark on Midtown. The diversity and energy of Midtown also set the stage for twenty-first century creative industries and modes of cultural production, whose workers prefer an environment closer to Java City's sidewalk café than a button-down suburban office complex.[115]

This exuberant diversity drew young artists and creative people, but their efforts were not always well received by city government. Young Sacramentans resisted John Misterly's style of law enforcement, zoning codes that made buildings easier to destroy than repair, limitations on where young people could dance and play music, even rules prohibiting café seating on sidewalks. A new generation of city council members, elected directly by their neighborhoods, helped promote city life and support for artists by listening to their constituents.

Java City's original Eighteenth and Capitol café and its enormous camphor tree in 2012, shortly before the café's closure and the removal of the tree. *Photo by Tara Elizabeth.*

The people drove change, and when government listened, the neighborhood prospered. When they ignored the people's voice, the neighborhood suffered. This view challenged the old order's idea that Sacramento's soul was lost in a tide of postwar change, leaving a centerless city. The creative soul of Midtown brought the city back to life.

Notes

Introduction

1. Terry Whittier, "Trekkers vs. Trekkies," *Stardate* 7, January 24, 1976, 3.
2. Bruce Pierini, "Midtown's Mid-Life Crisis," *Sacramento Bee*, January 24, 1988, Forum 1.
3. Tim Holt, "Where's Suttertown?" *Suttertown News* 4, no. 21 (December 30–January 12, 1979): 2.
4. Richard Lloyd, *Neo-Bohemia: Art and Commerce in the Postindustrial City* (New York: Routledge, 2006), 63–70.
5. Joan Didion, "Notes from a Native Daughter," *Slouching Towards Bethlehem: Essays by Joan Didion* (New York: Farrar, Straus and Giroux, 1968), 171–85.
6. Brian Roberts, "Sacramento Since World War II," master's thesis, California State University, Sacramento, 1986, 22–28.
7. Didion, "Notes from a Native Daughter," 178.
8. Lloyd Bruno, *Old River Town* (Dunsmuir, CA: Suttertown Publishing, 1995), 69–73.
9. "KDVS History," kdvs.org/about/history (accessed June 1, 2014).
10. Ken Goffman, *Counterculture Through the Ages* (New York: Villard, 2005), 321–23.
11. *Sacramento Union*, "Butz Closes Campus to Chicago 7 Member," May 26, 1970, A1; Michael Fallon, "Butz Overruled—Hayden Speaks," *Sacramento Union*, May 27, 1970, A1; William Burg, *Sacramento Renaissance: Art, Music and Activism in California's Capital City* (Charleston, SC: The History Press, 2013).

12. Burg, *Sacramento Renaissance.*
13. Donald A. Dean, "Cocktails with Fonda," *Suttertown News*, September 16, 1975, 1.

Chapter 1

14. Search for term via NewsBank InfoWeb, infoweb.newsbank.com, May 9, 2014.
15. Divison of Research & Statistics, "Survey of Sacramento, California, Field Report Dated Dec. 2, 1938," Home Owners' Loan Corporation, 1938, accessed via http://salt.unc.edu/T-RACES website, May 23, 2014.
16. Clarence Caesar, "An Historical Overview of the Development of Sacramento's Black Community 1850–1983," master's thesis, California State University, Sacramento, 1985, 74–75.
17. William E. Mahan, "The Political Response to Urban Growth," *California History* (Winter 1990–91): 359–71.
18. Deb Marois, "An Economic History of Alkali Flat," unpublished paper, University of California–Davis, March 2003, 25–31.
19. Walter Yost, "Gut-Level Politics," *Suttertown News*, November 7–14, 1991, 24.
20. Paula Boghosian and Don Cox, *Sacramento's Boulevard Park* (Charleston, SC: Arcadia Publishing, 2006).
21. "The CADA Story," accessed via www.cadanet.org, June 2011; Denis Bylo, interview with the author, May 2013.
22. Lorraine Dias Hebron, "Daisy's Legacy," *Golden Notes* 53, no. 2; Kay Movagero, "They Drove Off the Hookers," *Suttertown News*, March 6, 1981, 1.
23. Clare McKeon, "Rev. Falwell Challenged by Local Gays," *Suttertown News*, February 28, 1985, 3; Bill Lindelof, "Falwell's Unlikely Beneficiary Sitting Pretty," *Sacramento Bee*, December 15, 1986, B2; Robert Davila, "Lambda to Mark A Decade," *Sacramento Bee*, September 16, 1996, B1.
24. Anne Rudin, interview with the author, 2013.
25. Phil Isenberg, interview with the author, May 7, 2014.
26. David Covin, *Black Politics after the Civil Rights Movement* (Jefferson, NC: McFarland & Company, 2009), 79–84.
27. Covin, *Black Politics*, 97–104; Tim Holt, "Mayoral Fever," *Suttertown News*, August 16, 1975, 1.
28. Michael Andrew Clausen, "Lavender Heights," thesis, Chico State University, Chico, 1998, 133–43.

CHAPTER 2

29. Richard J. Brenneman, "Outspoken Ex-Sheriff John Misterly Dies," *Sacramento Bee*, August 29, 1983, A1.

30. Unclassified file via vault.fbi.gov/malcolm-little-malcolm-x/malcolm-little-malcolm-x-hq-file-06-of-27, "Muslim Files Appeal Notice," *Sacramento Union*, July 27, 1961, 10.

31. Warren Holloway, "Outlaw Cyclist J.T. (Mother) Miles Makes Scene Last Time—in Hearse," *Sacramento Bee*, January 14, 1966; Hunter S. Thompson, *Hell's Angels* (New York: Ballantine, 1966), 42, 108, 337–43.

32. Kris Holloway, "Controversy Arises over Coffee House," *Branding Iron* 14, no. 5 (February 14, 1969): 3.

33. Jack Woodard, "The Misterly Years," Parts I, II and II, *Sacramento Union*, May 27, 28, 29, 1970.

34. *Sacramento Union*, "County Free of Vice, Gambling: Misterly," May 28, 1970; ibid., "Answers Those Who Fault John Misterly," May 28, 1970; Tom Horton, "Losing City Pride," *Sacramento Union*, May 28, 1970.

35. Tom Borgsdorf, Facebook group Things I Remember Growing Up in Sacramento.

36. Hoyt Elkins, "35 Arrested after Raid in County Park," *Sacramento Union*, March 16, 1970, A1; *Sacramento Bee*, "Carmichael Raid Turns into Melee," March 16, 1970, A1.

37. David Rolin, interview with the author, April 22, 2014.

38. Ricardo Villanueva, "Boulevard Nights," *Sacramento Magazine* (January 1982): 40–47.

39. William Burg, *Sacramento's K Street: Where Our City Was Born* (Charleston, SC: The History Press, 2012), 121.

40. *Eugene Register-Guard*, "Bottomless Dancing Ruled Not Obscene," July 16, 1969, 11A; *Watertown Daily Times*, "Bottomless Case Tried," August 27, 1969, 25; *Watertown Daily Times*, "Bottomless Dancing Lewdity or Nudity?" August 27, 1969, 7; *Anniston Star*, "Dancer Suzanne Haines Presents Her Case, Jury in Lewd Dance Case Gets a Look at Evidence," September 19, 1969, 5; *Lodi News-Sentinel*, "Sacramento Judge Back at the Bar Watching Go-Go," September 23, 1969, 3; *Charleston Daily Mail*, "Judge Earl Warren Jr. Accused of Forcing Not Guilty Verdict," October 3, 1969.

41. David Houston, interview with the author, May 15, 2014; Jackson Griffith, "Evolver," *Sacramento News & Review*, March 27, 2003.

42. Jodette Silhi, interview with the author, April 21, 2014; Bill Lindelof, "One Last Free Meal Served at Café Morocco," *Sacramento Bee*, June 10,

1991, B1; Bob Sylva, "She's Back in the Business of Life," *Sacramento Bee*, April 4, 1993, D3; Emily Page, "Best Belly Dancer with a Heart of Gold," *Sacramento News & Review*, September 27, 2007.

CHAPTER 3

43. Paula Boghosian, *Draft EIR: Crocker Annex Demolition* (Sacramento: Historic Environment Consultants, 1978), 13–25; KD Kurutz, "Sacramento's Pioneer Patrons of Art: The Edwin Bryant Crocker Family," *Golden Notes* 31, no.1 (Spring 1990): 11–31.
44. Oral history with Otis Oldfield, May 21, 1965, accessed via www.aaa.si.edu/collections/interviews/oral-history-interview-otis-oldfield-13601.
45. Boghosian, *Draft EIR*, 25–26; *Weird Tales* reference via tellersofweirdtales.blogspot.com/2011/10/harry-noyes-pratt-1879-1944.html.
46. Boghosian, *Draft EIR*, 90–91.
47. Oral history with Otis Oldfield; William Mahan, "Taxpayer Support for Art? The Federal Arts Project in Sacramento: 1937–41" *Golden Notes* 40, no. 3 (Fall 1994): 4–12.
48. Mahan, "Taxpayer Support for Art?" 14–25.
49. Stan Lunetta, interview with the author, February 2013.
50. Loren Means, "Stan Lunetta," *Ear* 9, no. 1 (February 1981).
51. *Suttertown News*, "Art from Chicano 'Air Force,'" August 27, 1982, 1; Tim Holt and Richard Bammber, "La Raza," *Suttertown News*, December 5, 1985, 1; Brenda Williams, "Keeping the Faith," *Suttertown News*, March 8, 1990, 6; Esteban Villa, interview with the author, June 9, 2014.
52. Villa, interview with the author; Phil Isenberg, interview with the author May 7, 2014.
53. Socorro Zuniga, interviews with the author, March 2013–April 2014; *Voces de la Mujer*, event program, CN Gorman Museum, UC Davis, April 14, 1996; *Mujeres Chicanas*: Creating Our Own Myths and Legends, event program and catalogue, Copy Graphics Center, CSU–Sacramento, 1997.

Chapter 4

54. Jane Jacobs, *The Death and Life of Great American Cities*, (New York: Random House, 1961), 187–88.

55. Lance Armstrong, "From Poverty to Riches: Sacramento Man Established Historical Eagle Winery," *Land Park News*, December 2011.

56. Sacramento city directories, 1910–1956.

57. Dick Baldwin, "The JayRob Theatre of Sacramento," unpublished paper, Sacramento State University, June 1, 1961, accessed via jayrobtheatre.wordpress.com.

58. Lesli Maxwell, "Actor Got His Start as Comic in Capital," *Sacramento Bee*, Saturday, November 26, 2005, A1; *Pasadena Independent Star-News*, "Pat Morita: The Hip Nip," January 22, 1967, 98–99.

59. Fred Nichols, "From Beats to Movies," *Suttertown News*, March 13–20, 1986.

60. Michael Pulley, "The Last Days of Victor Wong," *Sacramento News & Review*, October 18, 2001; Peter Haugen, "'Invasion' Recalls the Day When Martians Overran K-RAP," *Sacramento Bee*, Sunday, October 14, 1990.

61. Elizabeth Currid, *The Warhol Economy* (Princeton, NJ: Princeton University Press, 2007), 28–35.

62. Charles Johnson, "Going Under: Struggling Sacramento Gallery Fails to Master Art of Survival," *Sacramento Bee*, January 24, 1978, A11.

63. Maggie McGurk, "Tongue-in-Chic Affair," *Suttertown News*, May 29, 1981, 12; Susan Bryer, "Sacramento's Cult of the Absurd," *Suttertown News*, November 27, 1982, 2–3; *Suttertown News*, "Kafka Klatch," November 27, 1982.

64. Patricia Beach Smith, "Use Me: Art with a Purpose," *Sacramento Bee*, December 13, 1984, ST13; *Sacramento Bee*, "Art Walk Hits the Street Sunday," May 12, 1989, SC7; Dixie Reid, "Remembering Michael," *Sacramento Bee*, October 9, 2009, TK14.

65. *Sacramento Bee*, "Artist's Condition Serious after Attack; Show to Go On," September 17, 1985, B3; Richard Bammer, "Fred Uhl Ball, 1945–1985," *Suttertown News*, January 2, 1986.

66. Lillieanne Chase, "The Artist's Life," *Suttertown News*, November 28, 1980.

67. Ken Magri, "Plaza Park Goes Dada," *Suttertown News*, July 3, 1987, 2.

68. Oral history interview with Brian Gorman, May 15, 2013; Bob Sylva, "Life on the Fringe," *Sacramento Bee*, February 28, 1988; Aric Johnson and Winda Benedetti, "3-Alarm Fire Destroys Midtown Warehouse," *Sacramento Bee*, August 2, 1993.

69. Marione Ashburn, "New I.D.E.A. in Town," *Suttertown News*, March 21, 1985, 5.

70. Jill Estroff, "Tripled Rent Forces Gallery to Move," *Suttertown News*, March 13, 1986, 5.
71. Fred Nichols, "Midtown," *Sacramento Bee Magazine*, June 25, 1989, 9.

Chapter 5

72. Walter Yost, "Gut-Level Politics" *Suttertown News*, November 7–14, 1991, 24.
73. Neil Matsuoka, "Who Owns Sacramento?" *Suttertown News*, January 23, 1976, 2.
74. Kenneth Jackson, *Crabgrass Frontier* (New York: Oxford University Press, 1985), 196–212; Sacramento redlining map accessed via T-RACES website, http://salt.unc.edu/T-RACES.
75. Jim and Delphine Cathcart, interview with the author, June 1, 2014.
76. Susan Larson, interview with the author, May 29, 2014.
77. Sacramento Branch of the American Association of University Women, *Vanishing Victorians* (Sacramento: Fong & Fong, 1973).
78. Bob Sylva, "Guts and Glory on I Street," *Sacramento Bee*, December 6, 1991.
79. Robin Datel, "Historic Preservation and Neighborhood Change in Sacramento, California," thesis, University of Minnesota, Minneapolis, 1978, 138, 100–01.
80. Datel, "Historic Preservation," 204–12, 214–19.
81. *Los Angeles Times*, "A Neighborhood Affair," July 26, 1981, Home 8.
82. Tim Holt, "Going, Going, Gone!" *Suttertown News*, September 12, 1991, 4.
83. Ibid., "Old City Group vs. 'Demolition Dave,'" *Suttertown News*, January 12, 1989, 3.
84. Pierini, "Midtown's Mid-Life Crisis," 3.
85. Robin Datel and Dennis Dingemans, "Historic Preservation and Social Stability in Sacramento's Old City," *Urban Geography* 15, no. 6 (1994): 565–87.

Chapter 6

86. Scott Soriano, "The Valley," scene report, *MAXIMUMROCKNROLL* 23 (March 1985): 23.
87. Joan Didion, "Slouching Towards Bethlehem," *Slouching Towards Bethlehem*, 85.

88. Michael Azerrad, *Our Band Could Be Your Life: Scenes from the American Underground 1981–1991* (New York: Little, Brown & Co, 2001), 122–33.

89. Dennis Yudt, "Sacramento's Underground Music from A–Z," *Midtown Monthly* (October 2011): 36–41; Andrea Juno and V. Vale, *Incredibly Strange Music*, Vol. 1 (San Francisco, CA: RE/Search, 1993), 6–12.

90. William Fuller, "Remembrance of Things Cell," liner notes from *The Parabolic Rock: 1975–1982* (Sacramento: SS Records, 2010); Tim McHargue, "The Music Scene," *Suttertown News*, May 16, 1980; Martin Cohen, "Life after New Wave," *Suttertown News*, May 4, 1980.

91. Dennis Yudt, interview with the author, May 14 2013; Kevin Seconds, interview with the author, April 19, 2014.

92. Gary Brown, "Old Auto Row on K Street Needs Touch of Cinderella," *Sacramento Union*, September 20, 1969, C11; Glenn Coin, "Downtown Residents Battle Hookers," *Suttertown News*, April 12–19, 1984, 1.

93. Ken Chavez, "Georgian Gives Up Fight, Shuts Cardroom for Good," *Sacramento Bee*, July 13, 1990, B6.

94. Ron Borges, "New Boxing Promoter on Scene," *Sacramento Union*, December 31, 1977, F4; Juleigh Howard Hunt, "Punk Promoter" *Suttertown News*, June 6, 1985, 5; Stewart Katz, interview with the author, May 20, 2013.

95. *Suttertown News*, "Punk Club Closed by Cops," July 29, 1983, 2; Pam Slater, "Punk Club Owner Sues City over Shutdown," *Sacramento Bee*, July 29, 1983, B9; Bob Sylva, "Punk Pride Takes to Streets," *Sacramento Bee*, July 28, 1983, D4; Kathryn Perkins, "Punk Rock Fans Protest Dance Laws," *Sacramento Bee*, July 30, 1983, B1; *Sacramento Bee*, "Club Minimal Gets Dance Permit," August 5, 1983, C4.

96. Stewart Katz, interview with the author, May 2013; Sumpy, "Stu Katz," *SPAMM Zine* 5 (July 1984).

97. Chris Macias, "A Hip Heritage," *Sacramento Bee*, June 25, 1999; Sumpy, "Rat's Ass of the Tales of Terror," *SPAMM Zine* 4 (circa 1984); Guphy Gustafson, "Tales of Terror," *Midtown Monthly* (January 2010).

98. Tim McHargue, "A New Wave Baptism," *Suttertown News*, April 27, 1980, 6; Elayne Wilson-Wallis, "New Wave Entrepreneur," *Suttertown News*, May 4, 1980; "City Won't Bare It," *Sacramento Magazine* (January 1982): 12.

99. Quote from David Barton, "Spanky's Works the Crowd," *Sacramento Bee*, October 12, 1986; David Watts Barton, "Innovative and Jazzy Experiment," *Sacramento Bee*, April 14, 1985; Bob Sylva, "A Nightclub Rises from the Shell of a Derelict Theater," *Sacramento Bee*, March 11, 1984; Debbie Seusy, "Club Can't Tell: New Vigor for K St. Mall," *Suttertown News*, October 4, 1984, 16.

100. Susan Bryer, "Oasis Neighborhood No Paradise," *Suttertown News*, October 15, 1982; Tim Holt, "Nightclub's Neighborhood Problems," *Suttertown News*, February 27, 1986; Cecilia Chan, "Neighbors Blast Oasis at City Hearing," *Suttertown News*, July 3, 1986; Tim Holt, "The Oasis Goes Under," *Suttertown News*, July 24, 1986.

101. Music listings, *Suttertown News*, November 19, 1987.

102. City of a Beer: Sacramento Inbred Brand Project, nokilli.com/inbred/index.html.

103. Yudt, "Sacramento's Underground Music from A–Z," 36; Craig Usher, interview with the author, June 11, 2014.

Chapter 7

104. Ray Oldenburg, *The Great Good Place* (New York: Marlowe & Company, 1989).

105. Nancy Skelton, "Goodbye to Falor's," *Sacramento Bee*, May 28, 1975.

106. Tim Holt, "Coffee & Pastry," *Suttertown News*, October 31, 1975, 1.

107. Sacramento city directories, 1973–1977; Gerald H. Thomas, "A Brief History of the Coffee Wars of Sacramento," *North State Review* (August 2013): 5; Roger Lathe, "Downtown Cafés Delight Coffee Lover," *Sacramento Bee*, February 18, 1988, 1.

108. Laurence Press, "The Dedicated Diner: Pava's," *Mom…Guess What!* (July 1981): 4; Judy Tachibana, "Fire Guts Midtown Restaurant," *Sacramento Bee*, June 30, 1990, B3.

109. Tim Holt, "A Dream Deferred?" *Suttertown News*, March 22, 1984, 1; Tim Holt, "Eye Dream Still Hanging in There," *Suttertown News*, May 3, 1984; *Suttertown News*, "Local Politicos Move to Save Ice Cream Parlor," May 10, 1984; Joseph Abril, "The Final Soiree at Eye Dream Café," *Suttertown News*, June 21, 1984, 1.

110. Art Luna, interview with the author, 2011; Sue Ellen Ehrmann, "Luna's," *Suttertown News*, March 2, 1985.

111. Joan Riordan, interview with the author, April 23, 2013.

112. *Sacramento Bee*, "Capitol Garage," September 13, 1987, TK18.

113. Cathleen Ferraro, "Greta's Café in Midtown Closing," *Sacramento Bee*, April 6, 2000, E1.

114. Jo Ashburn, "The City's Specialty Bookstores," *Suttertown News*, August 6, 1983, 4.

115. Jacobs, *Death and Life of Great American Cities*, 150–51; Lloyd, *Neo-Bohemia*, 244–45.

Index

About the Author

William Burg was born in Skokie, Illinois, but he moved to California in 1973 when his father was accepted to graduate school at UC Davis. Burg attended Humboldt State University, becoming involved in the punk scene and writing *No Scene Anywhere*, a 'zine of music and coffee. After returning from college in 1991, he moved to Midtown in 1993, spending inordinate amounts of time in coffee shops. In 1995, he formed *Uberkunst*, a noise/performance art group, playing throughout northern California and at Sacramento's annual Norcal Noisefest. He became executive  director of the Noisefest in 2000. In 2003, he became interested in local history and neighborhood activism, returning to college and graduating from Sacramento State University's public history program in 2010. He joined Sacramento Old City Association in 2007 and became president in 2012. *Midtown Sacramento* is his sixth book about Sacramento.

Visit us at
www.historypress.net
....
This title is also available as an e-book